No More *Guilt*

Ten Steps
to a
Shame-Free Life

Douglas H. Ruben, Ph.D.

Mills & Sanderson, Publishers
Bedford, MA • 1993

Published by Mills & Sanderson, Publishers
41 North Road, Suite 201 • Bedford, MA 01730-1021
Copyright © 1993 Douglas H. Ruben

Library of Congress Cataloging in Publication Data

Ruben, Douglas H.
    No more guilt : ten steps to a shame-free life / Douglas H. Ruben
      p. cm.
    Includes bibliographical references and index.
    ISBN 0-938179-35-7 :
    1. Guilt. 2. Shame. 3. Interpersonal relations. 4. Self
-actualization (Psychology) 5. Behavior therapy.   I. Title.
BF575.G8R83 1993
152.4--dc20
                                     93-4340
                                       CIP

Printed and manufactured by Capital City Press.
Cover design by Triad Communications.

Printed and Bound in the United States of America

To laugh is to risk appearing the fool,
To weep is to risk appearing sentimental,
To expose your feelings is to risk exposing your true self...
But only the person who risks is *free*.

To my wife,
Marilyn

Other Selected Titles by Douglas H. Ruben

Bratbusters: Say Good-bye to Tantrums and Disobedience
Skidmore-Roth Publishers (1992)

Family Addiction: An Analytical Guide
Garland Press (1992)

Avoidance Syndrome: Doing Things Out of Fear
Warren H. Green, Publishers (1992)

Behavioral Handbook: Rapid Solutions to Difficult Behavior
Best Impressions International (1988)

Self-Control: A Programmed Text
Best Impressions International (1986)

Drug Abuse and the Elderly: An Annotated Bibliography
Scarecrow Press (1984)

CONTENTS

Foreword vii
From the Author ix

STEP 1: What Is Guilt? 1
  * What guilt really is

STEP 2: How to Spot Guilt 9
  * Why do you feel ashamed?
  * What people do to make you feel guilty
  * Why do you believe you are guilty?
  * Your guilt profile: "Is this really me?"

STEP 3: No More Taking It Personally 27
  * How you read meaning into actions
  * How to stop "reading into" actions
  * Roadblocks to look out for

STEP 4: No More Avoidance and Escape 39
  * What is avoidance and escape?
  * Solving avoidance and escape

STEP 5: No More Fear of Rejection 67
  * Facing the need for hurt
  * Risking disapproval
  * Letting it go—Detachment
  * Why rejection doesn't equal abandonment
  * Basic relaxation when feeling rejected

STEP 6: No More Fear of Failure 81
  * You've been caught!
  * Why perfectionism doesn't work
  * Exposing vulnerability in risk situations
  * Accepting and soliciting compliments
  * Reversing the impostor situation

STEP 7: No More Toxic Shame 101
         * When is it okay to be *wrong?*
         * When is it okay to be *bad?*
         * When is it okay to be *defiant?*
         * When is it okay to be *independent?*
         * It is important to go through these steps

STEP 8: No More Need for Control 117
         * Why controlling is really protecting
         * Sharing control

STEP 9: No More Feeling Hurt for Other People 143
         * Why feeling sorry is really the result of fear
         * Absorbing feelings

STEP 10: No More Repeating Bad Relationships 151
         * Stop sign on "comfortable" relationships
         * The separation trap
         * The rebound trap
         * Separation and divorce
         * Criteria for selecting new relationships

Recommended Reading 185
Index 187

Foreword

I would like to introduce you to Dr. Douglas Ruben, the author of this book. I mean, I would REALLY like to introduce you to him, in person. I know you would instantly be taken with him.

His smile and effervescent attitude reflect his deeply felt optimistic viewpoint of life and it is certainly most infectious. It is darn hard to walk away from any encounter with him and feel worse than you did before. You really have to work at it.

That's why this book is powerful. It's not just one of those *feel good* positive thinking things. Yes, those things are good for the moment. However, here you will find tools, methods, and techniques you will easily be able to take along with you into the *real* world. The world of guilt and shame.

It gets messy in that world. Emotional complications can sabotage your thinking and lower your self-esteem. So, how do you get through these complications? *Wishing* you'd be better won't work—neither will any gimmicks, tricks, or good deeds. These are only temporary band-aids, with no lasting effect. You want what *works and can stick with you forever.* You want healthier thinking. You want a guilt-free mindset. And, in order to get from Point A to Point B, you have to do what you usually do when you get lost. You either ask for directions from someone who knows the way, or you consult a road map.

Here, you have the road map drawn by someone who really knows the territory. Dr. Ruben's insight into behavior, both internal and external, is incisive and yet entertaining in his own unique way. He will show you how to avoid detours, find the most direct route and enjoy the changes in yourself along the way. You will find the REAL reasons for your feelings and behaviors and specifically what to do about them, step by step.

Each chapter gives you a gift. This gift is the restoration of control and power to you. You've probably been without that control and power long enough, maybe since childhood. Now you get it back and learn how to keep it. You'll resist feeling shame and embarrassment, and will stop perceiving yourself as a victim. You won't be a victim anymore after reading this book.

You'll feel reborn, full of vitality and ready to step forward and risk the *new you* whenever you get a chance. The feeling will be exhilarating.

I'll tell you why I know this. I've had the pleasure of appearing with Dr. Ruben on television shows across the country a number of times in my career. Two things have always been rather obvious to me: his vast experience and knowledge of human behavior, and his ability to communicate it most effectively. With this book, now you get the benefits of both his knowledge, which, by the way, helps thousands of people in his private practice, and his way of making it easily understandable. I personally have seen his methods work most delightfully over and over again.

I'm glad that you have joined us for this trip into change in your life. Fasten your seat belts, this journey can be exciting. Positive change can always be exciting.

I wish you well.

Damon Reinbold
Damon & Associates

Damon Reinbold, a Certified Hypnotherapist, is one of the world's foremost experts on hypnosis. He has been in private practice over 20 years and has flown to all parts of the country to teach such celebrities as Melanie Griffith, Don Johnson, Kathie Lee Gifford, and Sally Jesse Raphael (and many others) how to quit smoking, lose weight, gain confidence, and take control of their lives.

His expertise has been featured on such television programs as The Oprah Winfrey Show, The Tonight Show, 20/20, and many more. His skills have been recounted in publications like USA Today and Time Magazine, to name just two of many. His expertise lies in understanding and maximizing the use of the subconscious mind.

From the Author

Guilt. It's like a cold. It comes on suddenly. You sniffle; you cry; you feel confused. You feel strange all over. But that's only the beginning. Symptoms get worse. Slowly it seeps into your body, infecting you from the inside out. You're mood is a roller coaster; today happy, tomorrow depressed. Every day is different, and people around you can't figure it out. You say you're fine, but you know the truth; you're not fine. You're scared. Inside your thoughts are spinning; no one thought makes sense. All you know is this: You can't stop yourself from thinking *you're a horrible person and you do horrible things.*

This is the insidious cycle of guilt. A cycle that affects every sensitive person. Minutes, hours, days, even weeks are consumed fighting this cycle. But the battle is never over. Guilt is the normal cost of being yourself; of saying and doing things that upset people and cause arguments. Angry people hate you for being honest and loyal. They blame you for sharing personal thoughts and making them feel uncomfortable. People don't like your doing what they can't do. They don't like your being different, so have enough sense not to be different. Don't do anything they wouldn't do; *How dare you! You should fit in instead of sticking out like a sore thumb. C'mon, use your common sense!*

And so guilt is your red light. It warns you that you've gone too far. You've pushed a little too hard; you've reached your limit. You're too daring, too demanding, too confident, and, for heavens sake, you're way too intelligent. Guilt stops all these things. It's your last chance to stop doing *something bad* before you really cause major grief in the world. Warning lights flicker on and off shouting at you to change your behavior immediately. If you don't, the damage will be so severe, so irreversible, that nobody will ever like you again. You can't run, you can't hide; you can't even say you're sorry. There's no way out. It's your fault and you must feel shame. So, just face the music for being so self-centered and spoiling everything for everybody.

Is this really the way guilt attacks people? Does it follow the same cycle for every person? The answers depend on two things: *How afraid you are, and how good or bad your guilt-fighting skills are.* Did you grow up afraid of adults, afraid of friends, afraid of new situations—afraid to death of what people thought of you. Does all this describe you? Then you suffer extreme guilt. And what about your coping skills? Can you deal with conflict, criticism, and rejection? Do you freeze up when told you did something wrong? Or maybe you snap back and defend yourself. Either extreme means you're not sure how to react and you're relying on instinct. But instinct is failing you every time.

You're losing the battle with guilt because your fears and weak skills conspire against you. You get tired and want to give up. You never see the light at the end of the tunnel because too many obstacles block that light. The enemy is not *the people out there who make you feel guilty, but rather your own obstacles. Fear and weak guilt-fighting skills are those obstacles.*

If you are an adult who had or still has family members who are alcoholics, have explosive tempers, are non-demonstrative, or never talk to each other, guilt played a major role in your early years and may still be a problem today. This book is especially good for you.

No More Guilt means what it says. It's time to step back from the yo-yo cycle of being happy and sad after blaming yourself for everybody's problems. *No More Guilt* does this. It offers real skill-building strategies used by over 1,000 clients who suffered from guilt exactly the way you do. They were all ages, from all walks of life, and of both genders (guilt is not sexist). It affects everyone in the same way.

The ten steps that follow offer you a solid handle on the toughest fight of your life. There's no telling when shame may strike again and you want to have the ammunition to nip it in the bud. Using these steps, I was able to do just that. You've heard the expression, "Everybody has a skeleton in their closet." Well, I'm no exception. You see, Lady Luck never visited my house. I was a tall, skinny kid growing up; and very sensitive about my body. Kids called me "string-bean" and the "greasers" pushed me around, trying to provoke a fight. I said "No," but they hit me anyway.

On the basketball team I was told the tallest player is the best player; well, hurray for tradition. I usually played second string. This happened with most of the sports I played. The more ashamed I felt, the stronger my parents pushed more sports on me.

They wanted me to try harder; I wanted to retreat. I knew I couldn't play well. The team knew it and I knew it; I felt like an impostor. Finally I did retreat from sports and tried theatre. Drama was therapeutic because it forced me to take risks by acting out words and feelings other people thought were silly. But there was nothing silly about it. That impostor feeling went away. So did my fear of hurting people. It was okay to let people get annoyed—even hate me if they wanted to.

Now, many years later, feelings of shame return once in a while, playing tricks on my perception of things. But when these feelings arise, specific steps instantly go into motion that block fear and allow me to calmly stay in the frenzied situation. That's how you'll feel after mastering the 10-step approach and realizing how easy guilt-control can be. Don't be fooled by how old you are, or how horrible your childhood was; it just means these steps will help you even more. So, go ahead. Get started making your life happier and guilt-free.

Douglas H. Ruben

Okemos, MI • 1993

STEP 1
What Is Guilt?

If love is "never having to say you're sorry," what is guilt? Just the opposite. Feeling compelled to always say you're sorry. Guilt is an obsessive feeling that nothing you do for yourself or other people is enough. You should have done it better, quicker, or like others told you to. That would have prevented making mistakes, and mistakes are absolute sins.

Guilt is the terrible plague of constantly owing people apologies for anything and everything you think, feel, and do. Who you do things with, why you do them, and where you do them are also under suspicion. The jury is always in session, debating your fate and ready to pronounce a verdict. And the verdict feels like a death sentence. Death row you could tolerate; you know the end is near. But stewing over what people think for days on end feels like an unending death sentence. The agony goes on forever. The punishment never fits the crime. But in your mental court room, judge and jury always treat you like the defendant; you're always fighting for your life.

The first step to getting rid of your guilt is knowing why you're always fighting for your life. Why you always feel guilt. Get the true facts and reasons why you've not been able to get rid of it on your own.

Guilt suffocates you by forcing self-doubt down your throat. Even when you say, "Okay, enough is enough," the pep-talk is short-lived. One criticism, conflict or rejection and you feel like jello. It happens that fast.

Bullets of disapproval shoot out of nowhere, catching you off guard. Snipers attack your soft, vulnerable, "Sure, I'll help you" side just when you feel cheerful—when you think you're pleasing everybody and everything. But your "happy-go-lucky" side gets sliced to pieces. Happiness gets squelched; you're left hating yourself, hating others, and wondering what you could have done to prevent this latest trauma.

Attacks of guilt are very regular, but frequently unpredictable. You're not exactly sure when the next one is coming. But rest assured, hardly a day passes without its fair share of guilt episodes. That is why you need to know exactly what guilt is—from top to bottom. Clearly defining guilt frees you from guessing you "got the bug" when really you feel something else. Guilt sufferers can't tell guilt from other sensations, because guilt is so rampant. If you are a longtime guilt sufferer, separating guilt from nonguilt is especially vital for you. So, let's get the facts right, once and for all.

What Guilt Really Is

Thoughts: Guilt is repeating wrong statements over and over that you learned as a child and that continue to guide your adult life.

Feelings: Guilt is sensing muscular tension, crying, fear and panic either before, during or immediately after interactions.

Behaviors: Guilt is reacting to your thoughts and feelings in extremes by either retreating and saying nothing, or aggressively defending yourself.

Guilt is set in motion the moment you wake up in the morning. But guilt is not an elusive, mysterious process. The nuts and bolts of guilt go like clockwork. The timing goes like this:

First: You say or do something (almost anything), either by yourself or around others.

Second: You immediately look around to check on people's reactions. Their words and body language are taken literally. You analyze anything and everything the person says, does, or could say or do. If you're alone, you look at yourself from a bird's-eye view: as if you were another person watching what you just said and did. How you believe others might react to you becomes as real as if somebody really was there watching you.

Third: You tell yourself why your behavior was foolish; why you were imperfect and incompetent. The rules you quote are not reminders; they are reprimands. You scold yourself for actions and words. Scoldings take the form of, "You should have...," "Why didn't you..." and always follow urgently with "From now on, you better..."

This is not a long process. Rules pass through you in seconds. They are fast and painful. And they always leave their mark: Shame.

Fourth: You try to get out of the situation. If you're around other people, your actions and words gracefully excuse you from causing other people grief. Or, you might get angry; you lose your temper and yell, call the person names or throw things. All of this is to escape your terrible feeling of humiliation. If you're alone, you cry, possibly shout out the names of people who caused you grief in the past, and you may even have a temper tantrum. In other words, you react alone as you would around people.

Fifth: Okay, you got out of the situation. You're safe, but not out of trouble yet. Now it's time to reflect upon what just happened. You do this in your private video room. You privately replay the tape of what you just said or did, over and over again. You picture yourself and the other people: what they said, how you replied, and what you *should* have done instead. Then you insert new dialogue, new blocking, and then scold yourself for what you did wrong and could have done right. You swear it will be different next time.

Sixth: Short reprieve. You have a temporary respite from guilt, but not from anxiety. This is the post-guilt reaction of wondering if another attack is around the corner, and whether you should prepare for it now by saying and doing things *in anticipation of the attack.* You're tuned in to the world; your mind is a short-wave radio scanning for any possible warning signs of guilt. You're body is an electric wire; you walk on egg shells. You tiptoe gently around people. You say what they want to hear, and speak only when spoken to. Be ready for anything. Expect everything.

Okay, so now you know guilt follows a weird order. Thoughts, feelings and behaviors are all synchronized to guilt situations. What are *guilt situations*? Do they sneak up like lions, stalking their prey before the attack? No, not really. Guilt situations are simpler than that. They don't exist as you think of them. You can't point a finger at a series of statements or actions people do and stereotype them as "guilt-provoking." That's hard to do because of the first rule.

RULE 1

Nobody causes your guilt. Guilt is not an external force intruding on your life. If it intrudes, it is because you mistakenly invite it into your world. You twist what people say and do, thereby causing your own guilt.

This statement sounds wrong, doesn't it? Intuitively you know, for a fact, that what your spouse says digs deeply into you. Your mother-in-law's biting remarks also have deep fangs. So, guilt *feels* external. But the only thing external is people's behavior. Your spouse, children, friends, and relatives display a wide variety of behaviors you probably label as *guilt-provoking*. Your spouse may accuse you of making watery potato salad. What could be worse? How obvious? "He made me feel guilty about my mistake. He always does that." An open and shut case of "he-started it." Period. End of discussion.

But, is it? That's the old-you talking. You're so positive he's the culprit that you think every other word out of his mouth is "You do this wrong and you do that wrong." Maybe he is a negative person, but he doesn't cause your guilt. You cause your own guilt; all he does is say things. You do all the rest. You slip into the trap of all six guilt reactions.

Still, what is it that he or other people do that triggers this guilt habit? Starters of guilt are words and actions that he doesn't just do to *you*; he does them to *everybody*. But these things apparently do not bother other people. You're the only one reacting with guilt, because other people realize these words and actions are garden-variety statements tolerated in everyday social situations. Not only does your spouse use them, but so does everybody. They are routine comments, gestures and facial expressions embroidered into the fabric of life. There's nothing abnormal about them; they're normal everyday occurrences. It becomes your responsibility to learn to accept these things as normal.

Some common behaviors in other people can provoke guilt. Among these guilt-provoking behaviors may be such things as accusing you of doing something wrong; blaming themselves for not living up to your expectations; blaming you for their not living up to your expectations; blaming you for not living up to your own expectations; getting angry or aggressive toward you; doing things behind your back, saying you can't do them; saying "anyone but you would have known better..."; doing something bad or stupid; asking why you did something; looking at you funny; or asking you to do something you don't want to do.

Just because these behaviors are normal doesn't make them necessarily *appropriate*. It may be normal to ask why someone always comes home late, and to express an opinion about it. We're all entitled to our opinions. However, some opinions are intrusive, negative, and hurtful. Still, they do not cause your guilt. You do that yourself. To make this point easier, think of it in terms of Rule 2.

RULE 2

It's normal for people to react in different ways to normal life experiences. It's how these actions are interpreted that counts. Other people's normal reactions don't cause guilt in normal people—even when that reaction is inappropriate. Don't mistake *normal* for right or appropriate.

So, if you get bent out of shape because your boss calls you lazy, remember, her remark is normal. Bosses all over the planet make these remarks. It's not just your boss. But, how appropriate is her remark? That's a different story. It may be inappropriate for any of several reasons. If so, it calls for your assertive reply. We'll see how to go about that in Chapter 4.

And if you still think this idea is crazy, get ready for the craziest idea of all. Not only is guilt your own doing, but you *like* feeling guilty. What? Like it? That's outrageous! No way. But hold on a moment. Don't get angry. Keep reading. I know this idea doesn't set right with you.

"How can I like feeling guilty, if I want to be guilt free?" It's easy. You've done it so long that it feels natural. You know what to say and what to do. It's second nature to you. You breathe, you eat, and you go through *guilt habits*. Guilt habits are instinctive reactions already tuned in and ready to run at a moment's notice. They are habits deeply interwoven into your personality since childhood. Some people are natural leaders, others are natural musicians; you're natural at feeling guilty.

In fact, life without guilt is hard to imagine. Guilt habits consist of fear, anxiety, self-doubts, avoidance and escape reactions, depression, and aggression. With them, your life takes upward and downward emotional cycles at the drop of a coin, but these cycles at least are *predictable*. You know when cycles begin and when they end. You know how painful cycles can be; and the ways to buffer the pain. You know how to fake feeling happy when guilt attacks you; and when to surrender to guilt. You've mastered guilt for survival, believing guilt will never go away. And now that all this may change—guilt can be eliminated—you shudder in fear. *What will I do without it?*

Guilt is your emotional companion through life's miserable obstacles. You get through them safely and unscathed if you adopt a routine strategy and switch to automatic pilot. But, try to break the habit and you feel resistance. *Why, for Pete's sake?* Habits protect you from your worst enemy: vulnerability. You'd go out of your way to prevent vulnerability. You'd say anything, do anything, even defend hated guilt habits, just to prevent people from seeing you look stupid, incompetent, or imperfect. That's why Rule 3 is here. It gives you permission to distrust life without guilt. It says it's okay to feel reluctant about making the changes described in this book. You're trying hard to change— that's good enough. You don't have to accomplish everything at once. You can move at your own pace.

RULE 3

You're up against guilt habits. Break the guilt habit by trying new strategies slowly. The more these strategies feel fake or phony, and (you think) look strange, the more confident you can be that they are working. But if you try new things that instantly feel natural and comfortable, beware lest old habits return. New strategies never feel natural and comfortable at first.

Overall, guilt starts and stops in six ways: (1) You react to a situation. (2) You inventory how other people reacted. (3) You tell yourself rules about being wrong and stupid. (4) You try to get out of the situation. (5) You re-play the situation, figuring out what you did wrong. (6) You think ahead about future mistakes; remaining on guard and anxious, and expecting the worst.

Your first tools to combat intuitive feelings of guilt are these three rules:
RULE 1: You cause your own guilt.
RULE 2: Don't mistake normal reactions for guilt-provokers.
RULE 3: Fight guilt habits.

Let these rules establish your mind-set. Ahead of you are the best years of your life, because guilt is on its way out. You're in charge. You are in control for the moment, but this guilt-control may feel strange and unfamiliar. You might think the habit-removal process is not working. It is. Don't be afraid. It's working just fine.

STEP 2
How to Spot Guilt

This is your first chance to feel *No More Guilt*. This chapter puts a microscope on your guilt habits so you know exactly what *not to do*. Patterns are made crystal clear. You can't miss them. But get ready for a strange experience. It may feel eerie reading about behavior patterns that describe you perfectly. You don't expect to see yourself profiled so accurately in a book. After all, your guilt is personal; it's a unique experience. But guilt also has many common denominators, especially among adult children of alcoholics and others from troubled families. So, don't be surprised if you see yourself more than once in the pages ahead.

Why Do You Feel Ashamed?

Do you do things that people say are bad? You're not sure, but everybody else is certain they're bad. Your boss thinks so; your friends think so—even your spouse thinks so. If it's not one thing, it's another—everything you do or say is bad. There seems no escape from it. Blame is everywhere.

You feel ashamed, humiliated, and annoyed at being a bad person. Are these the type of things you do?

DO YOU ...
- frequently get defensive?
- frequently get angry at other people?
- frequently get upset by others getting ahead?
- frequently complain about others?
- distrust everybody you are with?
- hate to try new things and lack initiative?
- find excuses to get out of things?

- depend on others for constant feedback?
- hate change?

These are some characteristics of feeling guilty. How many of these describe you? Very few of these, you say? C'mon—you must possess one or two of these traits? None fit? If one or two traits fit you it is probably because you're working hard to make them fit. Like rationalizing to yourself that you *must* fit some of these because you feel so ashamed all the time. Maybe you hear others accuse you of these traits and it becomes second nature to accept that this must be how you are.

Well, not exactly. Being a *guilty person* does not mean you really are guilty of anything. Nor does it mean other people's perception of you is correct. Here's proof: Take a look at the next series of statements and then decide if this list fits you better. Start it off by saying "I am ashamed because I ..."

- am always the last to complete jobs.
- am always angry at myself.
- never believe my life is good enough or passes inspection.
- never accept compliments or praise.
- can never relax because I'm always behind.
- always feel embarrassed or incompetent.
- never really know what I am doing.
- always feel nobody else likes me or is happy with my behavior.
- always discover mistakes I made after the fact.
- never have happy thoughts like other people.
- always, or nearly always, avoid conflict.

Does this list describe you better? I'll bet it does. There's a reason for that. The reason is that people who believe they are guilty are extremely afraid of hurting other people. So afraid that every instant of every moment of every day is spent anticipating who will hate you next. Who will expose your mistakes and make you the laughing stock of your home or workplace? You torture yourself into hating every detail of every bit of behavior, insisting to yourself that it cannot possibly be right. It must be wrong—it must be bad; you must have done *something* wrong.

Do you ever anticipate the following?
- What if I make an error.
- What if I cause somebody grief.
- What if I embarrass somebody.
- What if I ruin something.
- What if I look stupid.
- What if I lose control.
- What if I draw attention to myself.

And there's the scariest of all: I might be abandoned! How horrible; how absolutely demoralizing to be abandoned. Parents leave me. Friends leave me. Boyfriends or girlfriends leave me. Face it, nobody likes me. People will know that I never was, never will be, and never could be a good person.

When does it end? The answer lies within yourself. You can end it by learning specific ways to break the cycle of self-assigned guilt, and put an end to your continual need to prove yourself at fault. You're not a guilty person; only you can know that.

What People Do to Make You Feel Guilty

I'll bet you woke up this morning feeling ashamed. Families are notorious for making people feel ashamed. They don't do it deliberately, of course. Nobody does. But in the everyday course of events mistakes arise that are blamed on the weakest link. It's another example of Darwin's survival of the fittest. Those who fare best are those who do not get blamed. Those who are blamed struggle for survival.

Families looking for the weakest link prey on their scapegoat. This is the person most easily intimidated—the glutton for punishment. Youngest, oldest, middle child—it doesn't really matter. It's the child who can take the crass teasing, insults, and blame that gets whipped the most. Scapegoats usually have three things in common:

1. They are afraid of conflict.
2. They are rescuers who work hard at keeping the peace.
3. They are always doing things for others.

Call it caretaking, being overresponsible, or just plain unlucky, but scapegoats accept the guilt for other family members, thereby letting them off the hook. If you are the family scapegoat, here are some of the behaviors you may use— erroneously—to free parents and siblings from fault.

- apologizing all the time
- blaming yourself when it is clearly their fault
- disqualifying or criticizing yourself
- painting a rosy picture of a gloomy situation
- creating a fantasy of how it might be if things were perfect
- downplaying the seriousness of problems
- promising to resolve conflict when you have no intentions of doing anything

Why Do You Believe You Are Guilty?

Feeling guilty is the result of many past events. These events began in childhood. Young girls and boys observe that good people are those in authority—Mom and Dad—and that being like Mom and Dad feels "right." Failure to live like Mom or Dad or how you *expect* Mom and Dad would have you act, means you are bad. Pressure to live up to these expectations becomes the yardstick by which you judge everything you do.

Consider the community you grew up in. Was it an ethnic or religious community? Did you live by certain social customs? Or did you belong to a class of people having their own standards, rituals and expectations? Maybe all of these. How well did you fit into those expectations? An orthodox Jewish upbringing has strong indoctrination on what is right and wrong. So does a Catholic or Protestant upbringing. And so does social class—blue collar or white collar, it doesn't matter. How you should speak, sit, react, and who you should choose for a mate— all of this is taught. There is a right way and a wrong way. Or so it seems. Moderation is out of the question. You will do it *this* way and no other way, so help you God!

Details of your childhood pop up everywhere in your life. What you wear, what you eat, even your favorite movies: all shadings of childhood influence. You are the product of things taught to you over a long period of time. How well these things get you through life depends on how you approach challenges. An ambitious approach means you can be flexible; risk is okay and what people think about you is unimportant. A safe approach means the opposite. You're not flexible. You're ultra-sensitive to mistakes and highly critical of your faults.

It all starts in childhood. A guilty-person's image includes many of the following experiences. Mark an x next to the ones that fit you.

_____ Parents were very demeaning or punished you a lot.
_____ Parents insisted you'd never become anything in life.
_____ Parents fought like cats and dogs.
_____ Parents blamed you for their mistakes and fights.
_____ Mistakes you made were terribly criticized.
_____ Your peers were always "better than you."
_____ Good things you did were ignored or overlooked.
_____ Parents refused to hear your reasons.
_____ Parents told you not to "toot your own horn" (brag).
_____ Parents insisted you were no better than anyone else.
_____ Parents reminded you it is a lonely world and having friends is absolutely essential.
_____ Parents punished you for independence.

Spot quite a bit? Don't be surprised. These are common mistakes parents make that cause us to feel GUILTY. Guilt was convenient for parents who knew no other way of expressing anger other than taking it out on you.

If wrath and fury described your household, consider the form it took.

- Anger was random—you never knew when it would strike.
- Anger was explosive—it was here now and gone in moments.
- Anger was continuous—you never had a moment of peace.
- Anger was arbitrary—it either came as physical or verbal abuse.

- Anger was nondirective—anybody was fair game.
- Anger always accompanied criticism.
- Anger always signaled the worst was yet to come.

How many times do you remember hiding in your room, under the bed, or in the bathroom so that you could escape from anger. It was always there—following you around without leaving a hint as to when it would return. No clues, just surprises; bad surprises. Surprises that you were unprepared for because you lacked any way of coping with them. Anger in any form left you injured, paralyzed, and feeling entirely responsible for what happened. *It was your fault—forget why or how; you just knew you had to have done something wrong.*

That's all it took in childhood for you to feel everybody around you was a saint and you were the sinner. That's all it took to think your family was conspiring against you, because *you* were the freak. Complaints about who you were and what you did were valid. Your friends and family *knew* it then, so people must be right to blame you for mistakes today.

There's only one problem with this conclusion: Who says your family and friends were right? When you feel guilty you may be reacting to a history full of people treating you like you're guilty.

This has continued in every phase of life: from school to meeting new people, to starting a career. Stumbling from one problem to another problem; from one bad relationship to another bad relationship, you doubted every move you made. But it wasn't you making the bad moves. It was other people who made the bad moves and couldn't swallow the hurt that went along with them. So they got rid of their hurt. They shoved it onto you. You became the garbage dump of their problems. What's worse, you never had anybody to pass your problems on to. And you didn't know how to give the problems back to their original owners. So guess who was out of luck?

Right. You again.

Your Guilt Profile: "Is This Really Me?"

Okay, for the moment let's say this really is you. You get caught in the trap of guilt habits. All day long, habits control everything you do. It's like breathing.

You enjoy doing things for people. This means you:
- Do what people say to do.
- Compromise your needs for those of other people.
- Think nothing of being selfless; the more you do for others, the more moral you feel.
- Love to listen to people. You absorb their words and grief, and sink into their problems as if they were your own.

You lose your temper around people. This means you:
- Get upset when you don't know how to do some thing.
- Get upset when you make a mistake. You blame other people for the mistake.
- Get upset thinking you're about to be criticized; you zap the critic before he or she zaps you.
- Get upset to escape a sensitive or intimate situation you feel will make you look stupid.
- Get upset when other people are running the show; it's scary to be a leader, but it's worse being out of control.

You get anxious and panicky. This means you:
- Get anxious if you feel pressure or think conflict is around the corner—much like a barometer.
- Feel panic when you can't avoid, can't escape, and don't know what to do under pressure or conflict.
- Feel about to be humiliated, embarrassed or criticized.

You don't say anything. This means you:
- Get out of situations.
- Stay real quiet so nobody gets angry with you.
- Can't look somebody in the eyes.
- Feel on the verge of crying.

You run away. This means you:
- Literally go somewhere else when you feel upset.
- Might hop in the car and just drive.
- Might run to a friend's or sibling's house—sometimes even to your parents.

You abuse substances. This means you:
- Drink beer or mixed drinks, smoke cigarettes or marijuana, or use other chemicals when feeling bad.
- Get high, or "take the edge off" when feeling nervous and scared.
- Enjoy drinking or smoking because it lets you be a different—guilt-free—person.

You feel emotionally paralyzed. This means:
- You panic when you feel helpless or think you did something wrong.
- You remain still, saying nothing, doing nothing—you feel your whole body go numb.
- All you can think about is how horrible you are and what your punishment will be.

You suddenly are very attentive. This means you:
- Become keenly aware of everything around you. What people say, how they look at you. What they smell like. What they wear. What they're not wearing. Little cues are spotted. Your antenna are up, scanning anything you think is important.
- Think quickly, like you have two seconds to defuse an explosive. One-hundred percent attention is on what you're doing. No distractions.
- Feel in touch with bodily sensations. Pains, aches, twitches and itches are all monitored closely. You keep close tabs on your body in case *something goes wrong*—like you have a panic attack. You believe that keeping a close watch on your inner body will *prevent* anxiety or panic. But it really doesn't. Anxiety or panic occur

anyway. You're actually bringing it on faster by waiting and watching for it.

You're passive. This means you:
- Say nothing and look friendly when somebody is angry with you.
- Wait for the anger, criticism, disapproval, or conflict to go away.
- Start a pleasant topic, trying to distract the arguer. You'll ask the arguer about good things that happened in his or her day.
- Say, "I'm sorry." It becomes habitual. You'll apologize repeatedly. You won't even know what you're apologizing for. It doesn't matter. And you don't care. You just want the anger and conflict to stop.
- Make the arguer feel good. This happens many ways. You'll do all sorts of things: buy gifts, cook meals, make up compliments, have sex, and agree to whatever the person asks you to do. It makes you feel better. And you think the angry person feels better too.

You're full of revenge. This means you:
- Get angry later. Hours after a conflict you take out your frustration on your daughter, son, pet, or best friend. You can't believe how scary you get. It's Dr. Hyde from Hell. You spew mean words and threats all over the place. Then you attack the walls, drawers, and other objects. You may even destroy things. Your favorite things. If it's small, it can fly. And you'll throw it, kick it, or tear it up.
- Get revenge. Not during the conflict, but *afterwards*. And it's not impulsive. You're methodical. Carefully crafted efforts go into upsetting a person. You'll conspire all sorts of things: hide the person's possessions, ruin a meal, *conveniently* forget to relay telephone messages, leak air from their tires, or tell lies. There's no end to your conniving obsessions. Adrenaline pumps as you think up new forms of vengeance. You reach euphoria when the

person is caught off guard. They weep, get angry, and suffer from not knowing who did it and why it happened. But you know. And you love every minute of it.

You pretend you don't know anything. This means you:
- Say, "I don't know," or "I have no idea what you're talking about." But that's a lie. You know exactly what the person is talking about. You just keep it to yourself.
- Offer sympathy, or politely listen to the nasty person huff and puff over something you did or something that happened. You put on a "happy smile" while mumbling "go to Hell" under your breath.

You feel like an impostor. This means you:
- Think people can look right through you and see you don't know anything.
- Feel anxious speaking up in a group for fear of sounding stupid.
- Distrust good feelings. You feel that for everything good there will be horrible things around the corner. So, you're just waiting for the other shoe to drop. It's coming. You know it is. There's no way you feel you deserve a break in life.
- Can't talk, think or move an inch without being self-conscious. It's like an out-of-body experience. There you are, talking to other people, but you're not focusing on those people. Your mind is elsewhere. You're thinking about how you look, how you speak, and what people think about you.

You absorb people's problems. This means you:
- Feel what others feel. You step deeply into the person's life, experience their problems as if they were your own. It's like catching a person's cold. You catch a person's contagious problems.
- Volunteer your own faults as a sacrifice to make a sad or angry person feel better. You put yourself down—way down—because you get your pleasure from seeing other people happier than you are.

You feel depressed. This means you:
- Tell yourself you're a bad person.
- Stay home and don't do anything.
- Always feel tired, bored, or useless.
- Think how much happier others would be without you.
- Think you're ugly.
- Stop eating or eat poorly.
- Feel desperate for a quick fix to feel happy.

By now you have probably figured out that guilt is a real thing. You really *feel* it and *act* in guilty ways. Guilt will not simply go away after you reach a certain age. It stays with you. It gets worse and seizes the best years of your life. That's why you're going to stop it—*now*. Put all of your thoughts together. Step back and really look at yourself in view of the patterns described so far. You're ready for your first test. The odds are even. It's you against you. Find out once and for all how much guilt you really carry around.

Read the questions below and circle *true* or *false*. Then, at the end, add up your scores for each category. A chart will help you pinpoint where you stand on the guilt profile.

GUILT PROFILE TEST

Feelings (F)
1. Do you have trouble saying what's on your mind?
   TRUE   FALSE
2. Do you think your ideas will impose on others?
   TRUE   FALSE
3. Do you believe your ideas are stupid or people will hate them?
   TRUE   FALSE
4. Do you edit your thoughts in your mind before saying them?
   TRUE   FALSE
5. After you say things, do you stew over what you said and how people probably reacted to it?   TRUE   FALSE
6. Do you get angry real fast if you speak your mind?
   TRUE   FALSE

7. Do you get angry if you are criticized?
   TRUE   FALSE

8. Do you feel that sharing personal information allows others to see your weaknesses?   TRUE   FALSE

9. Do you provoke your spouse or partner just to end arguments?
   TRUE   FALSE

10. Do you think looking weak means people will exploit you?
    TRUE   FALSE

11. Do you feel people can look right through you and think you don't know what you're talking about?
    TRUE   FALSE

12. Do you end friendships if you're angry at your friend?
    TRUE   FALSE

Relaxed (R)

1. Do you find it hard to enjoy idle time?
   TRUE   FALSE

2. Is it difficult to sit and do nothing while watching TV?
   TRUE   FALSE

3. Does doing nothing make you feel guilty?
   TRUE   FALSE

4. Does doing nothing make you feel nervous or afraid?
   TRUE   FALSE

Loyal (L)

1. Once you say, "I'll do that for you," must you do it for them, no matter what?   TRUE   FALSE

2. Are you afraid to say "False"?
   TRUE   FALSE

3. Does how you feel depend on how much you do for others?   TRUE   FALSE

4. Do you hate people doing things for you?
   TRUE   FALSE

5. Is it hard to accept compliments?
   TRUE   FALSE

6. Do you put yourself down, but compliment others?
   TRUE   FALSE

Control (C)

1. Do you feel nobody can do things better than you can?
   TRUE   FALSE

2. Do you only trust yourself, not others?
   TRUE   FALSE

3. Is it hard to be a follower?   TRUE   FALSE

4. If somebody does things for you, do you feel it's because you can't do them yourself?   TRUE   FALSE

5. If somebody does things for you, do you feel you owe them something in return?   TRUE   FALSE

6. Do you hate surprises?   TRUE   FALSE

7. Do you hate making changes?   TRUE   FALSE

8. Do you hate criticism?   TRUE   FALSE

9. When things don't go your way, do you blame yourself?
   TRUE   FALSE

10. If you blame other people for mistakes, do you feel guilty?
    TRUE   FALSE

Relations (RE)

1. Do you have to have an intimate relationship?
   TRUE   FALSE

2. Do you find yourself attracted to the same type of person?
   TRUE   FALSE

3. Do you feel paralyzed when partners break up with you?
   TRUE   FALSE

4. Is it easy to feel what others feel?
   TRUE   FALSE

5. Do you think living alone is a horrible thing?
   TRUE   FALSE

6. Do you find yourself in relationships with people who have problems?   TRUE   FALSE

7. Is it hard to end relationships when you know you should?
   TRUE   FALSE

8. When going out on dates, are you afraid of repeating old mistakes?   TRUE   FALSE

Drugs and Alcohol (D/A)
1. Do you drink a beer or mixed drink, or smoke marijuana every day?   TRUE   FALSE
2. Do you drink beer or mixed drinks, or smoke marijuana once a week?   TRUE   FALSE
3. When you're in a social situation, do you always have to drink or smoke something?   TRUE   FALSE
4. Does your spouse or partner drink or smoke something every day, on the weekend, or many days during the week?
                                                        TRUE   FALSE
5. Did a person in your family growing up have a problem with alcohol or drugs?   TRUE   FALSE
6. Do you smoke one to three packs of cigarettes a day?
                                                        TRUE   FALSE
7. Do you eat, drink or smoke when you feel nervous?
                                                        TRUE   FALSE
8. Do you eat, drink or smoke when you feel tired?
                                                        TRUE   FALSE
9. Do you eat, drink or smoke when you feel bored?
                                                        TRUE   FALSE
10. Do you have many major medical problems?
                                                        TRUE   FALSE

Fear (FE)
1. Are you afraid you might cause somebody grief?
                                                        TRUE   FALSE
2. Are you afraid you might embarrass somebody?
                                                        TRUE   FALSE
3. Are you afraid you might look stupid?
                                                        TRUE   FALSE
4. Are you afraid of mistakes?   TRUE   FALSE

Parents (P)
1. Did your parent(s) get angry "all the time"?
                                                        TRUE   FALSE
2. Did one of your parents have a quick temper?
                                                        TRUE   FALSE
3. Was one parent very critical and angry at you?
                                                        TRUE   FALSE

4. Did your parent(s) insist you'd never amount to anything?

   TRUE   FALSE

5. Did your parent(s) fight all the time?

   TRUE   FALSE

6. Did you have a real strong and real weak parent?

   TRUE   FALSE

7. Did your parent(s) blame you for their mistakes?

   TRUE   FALSE

8. Did you argue much with your parent(s)?

   TRUE   FALSE

9. Did your parent(s) ignore your good qualities?

   TRUE   FALSE

10. Did your parent(s) refuse to hear your reasons?

    TRUE   FALSE

11. Did your parent(s) never hug or kiss or show affection to you?

    TRUE   FALSE

12. Did your parent(s) say "don't think you're better than other people?"   TRUE   FALSE

13. Did your parent(s) say you must please other people?

    TRUE   FALSE

Score yourself

Now count up the number of *TRUE* items you circled under each category. Categories are abbreviated *F, R, L, C, RE, D/A, FE,* and *P*. Insert the number in the first space, next to the category. Now divide that number by the number in brackets, and multiply it by 100. This gives you a percentage score. Go ahead and try this part now.

SCORE:						
F ___	(12)	___%	RE ___	(8)	___%
R ___	(4)	___%	D/A ___	(10)	___%
L ___	(6)	___%	FE ___	(4)	___%
C ___	(10)	___%	P ___	(13)	___%

Once you have percentages, take your percentages for each category and plot them on the *Behavior Profile Chart* on the preceding page. Do this by marking the percentage for *F* under the column for *Feelings*. Mark the percentage for *R* under the column for *Relaxed*. Continue this for each column until you mark a percentage in each column.

Now look at the shaded areas at the bottom of the profile. These shaded regions signify the "okay" zone. There are two okay zones: a dark shaded portion and a light shaded portion. If all your marks fall in either of these shaded regions your guilt level is pretty normal and this book will fine tune what you already know about handling fear and anxiety.

But let's suppose you're not so lucky. Maybe one or two of your marks barely squeeze into the shaded okay zone, while the majority of your marks are scattered all over the chart. You have both high and low marks, and perhaps many marks are at the top, at 100%. That means guilt is winning in your life, and the help offered in this book can't come too soon. You're looking at how guilt runs your life in all these different categories. It will only grow more fierce unless you make use of the ten steps described in the pages that follow. *It's in your hands to turn your life around and make the rest of your years guilt-free.* So, let's turn the page and get started.

Behavior Profile

	Feelings	Relaxed	Loyal	Control	Relations	Drug/Alc.	Fear	Parents
100								
95								
90								
85								
80								
75								
70								
65								
60								
55								
50								
45								
40								
35								
30								
25								
20								
15								
10								
5								

STEP 3
No More Taking It Personally

Walking around like a live wire is awful. You feel plugged into everybody's thoughts. Your radar is on. And you scan everything you think people say or do: what they're thinking, what they're looking at, and why they're looking at it. It's buzzing all the time in your mind. It's like a loud radio. Sometimes you can turn it off when you're tired, angry, or laughing. Sometimes it just goes away on its own. But that's rare.

You see, *you can't afford to turn the scanner off because it is your only way to prevent feeling guilty.* Avoiding guilt involves being extra-alert to people around you so that you can anticipate conflicts, criticisms, and any problems making you feel inferior. Constant awareness keeps you on your toes. You're always on guard. The more you see, the more you hear, the more you know—the better you're prepared. You'll get them before they get you. Your guilt alarm is always on-call, ready to be turned on at a moment's notice, and your entire personality goes into remedial action.

Do you know why this happens? It's because you feel that everything you do *naturally* is wrong. Talking naturally is wrong. Smiling naturally is wrong. Walking naturally is wrong. There is no question in your mind. You don't *think* it's wrong, to you it *is* wrong. And so you believe people around you also perceive it as wrong. You're waiting for their disapproval by sizing up the situation and calculating how and why people perceive your action as wrong. This mental process goes on in great detail. It's more complex than a computer. In your mind you figure out several things all at once. It's not just "What are they thinking?" It is more like:

1. Why is she angry?
2. She only gets angry when such and such happens.
3. Did I do such and such?
4. I must have done something, and here's how it happened.
5. I could have done it this way, that would have been better.
6. Okay, what are the consequences for what I did?
7. What are the chances this bad thing will happen today, maybe tomorrow?
8. After it happens, what then? I don't know. I better run through that scenario in my mind.

Deduction after deduction. Speculation after speculation. It goes on and on and on. You work up a sweat from your mental gymnastics by probing every possible angle the situation may go in, graphically imagining it through colorful scenarios. You're staging the whole performance from start to finish—deciding who says things, when they will say them, and how you will respond to them. You're director, choreographer, and audience all in one. It all runs smoothly through your mental circuitry until there's a snag. Snags you can't figure out start a panic. "Oh my God, what am I going to do?" You rerun the scenarios, switch the dialogue, replay the action, and play it out again until it *feels right.* And you replay the scene over and over again, until you believe—with absolute certainty—that you can prevent conflict and the resulting shame.

The mind-games you go through are stressful. You work so hard internally at strategizing a win-win situation that you lose touch with life. Life seems awful because it's like a chess match. Every move takes twenty minutes to figure out. You concentrate on concentrating. Will it always be that slow? Or, can I ever go faster?

Yes, you can go faster. That's what this chapter is going to teach you. This is where you learn to recognize how you jump to conclusions by reading meaning into the actions of others, and how to stop doing it.

How You Read Meaning Into Actions

You read into people's actions by intuition. No, you're not psychic, although you probably feel you are. Yes, you've predicted things before. Yes, you sense things in the world that other people are completely oblivious to. And yes, you're like a thermometer. You always know when people will reach their boiling points. And why shouldn't you know this? Growing up, and as an adult, you've watched everything that happened around you to avoid getting into trouble. The more you tuned into life, the more control you felt. So, here's what you've done instinctively for a long time:

1. You watch and listen to people very closely. The more important they are to you, the closer you zero-in on them.
2. You say to yourself, "She's doing that for the same reason she's done it before." Whatever reason in the past accounted for her action is the reason you think she's doing it now.
3. You say to yourself, "Why would I do what she's doing?" Whatever reason you might have for doing what this person is doing, becomes her reason for doing it.
4. You say to yourself, "Is there somebody at fault here?" Sure there is. There's *always* somebody at fault when you think, eat and breathe guilt. You blame either yourself or the other person. If it's her fault, then you think "She should/could have done something differently" or "She always does this bad thing to me." If you blame yourself, then you think "I should/could have done something to prevent this—God I'm stupid."

Let's look again at all four steps in "reading into" actions:
1. Watch behavior.
2. Assume they're behaving the way they are because of something they did in the past.
3. Assume they're doing it for the same reasons you'd do it to them.
4. Assume they're to blame or that you're the one at fault.

You're assuming too much. Assumptions start from CSWs or COULD BEs, SHOULD BEs and WOULD BEs. They're not based in facts. Facts are skipped over because you think you have all the answers. You feel certain your reasons are truth. They feel true, so they *must* be true.

How to Stop "Reading Into" Actions

Can you stop the roller coaster ride before you get nauseous? Does it just go up and down forever? It has thus far, and probably will keep going until you push the *STOP* button. So, here's where you push that button.

You can prevent assumptions by taking simple steps as you read them on paper. Of course, nothing is *really* simple about them. They only sound simple because the steps are logical. And you're a whiz at logic. But when you know *what* to do and *how* to do it, fears about trying the steps will go away.

Basic steps to prevent assumptions

Only genies can look through crystal balls and foresee the future. But you can predict the future without a crystal ball by just sensing that mischief is around the corner. Of course, you're just guessing. Guesswork is loaded with assumptions piled high over time from trying to know everything and being certain about nothing. You can interrupt the flow of assumptions by following five steps:

STEP 1: *Look at only "what" the person is saying and doing, not "why" he is saying or doing it.*

Try this experiment for starters. Look at somebody right now. Watch his body motions. Now describe exactly what you see. Is he making faces? Is he moving his hands a lot? Describe physical movements in dry and simple terms. Such as: "He's laughing." "He's walking fast." "He's talking fast." "He's looking at a book." The more concretely you describe it, the better the description is.

Now for the verbal end of things. Try listening to what the person is saying to somebody else. Again, describe this action in very plain language. For example: "She's talking about shoes." "She's telling the other person what her mother did." *Why* this person is saying these things *is unimportant.* Stick with *what* is going on, not why. Don't read into it, under it, over it, or anything else about it except what you see or hear. Make no judgments.

STEP 2: *Think about what you see happening, don't assume you know anything about why it is happening.*

First you have to shift gears. You're so used to reading *why* into every situation you observe that ignoring the *why* seems wrong. But it isn't wrong. You only feeling it's wrong because you're doing something new. And new things never feel right.

Once you've learned not to *assume the why,* it's time to discover the true facts by *asking why.* To do this, describe the same action you did a moment ago, but this time put a *why* in front of it. Ask a question as if you were speaking to a person nearby. You'd ask, "Why are you laughing?" "Why are you walking fast?" "Why are you talking about your shoes?" "Why are you telling another person about your mother?" Direct, specific questions pointedly check out your facts.

STEP 3: *No facts, No fault (F&F).*

You're going to ask people questions because you don't know exactly why something is happening. And when you don't know the facts, don't blame yourself. That's called F & F; or no facts, no fault. If you don't have the facts, it's not your fault. You see, when somebody says or does something to you, ask yourself these questions and answer them a new way:

1. What am I assuming here? You're assuming you did something wrong.

   NEW ANSWER: I don't know what's going on here because I don't have the facts. And, no facts, no fault—F & F.

2. Why is the assumption wrong? It's wrong because you lack facts.

NEW ANSWER: Again, If I don't have the facts, it's not my fault—F & F.

3. Why am I a bad person? You're assuming you're bad because the person is talking to you and something *may be wrong*.

 NEW ANSWER: You're not bad. You're just not sure. It's okay to be unsure. Check out your facts.

4. Why am I better than others? I couldn't possibly be better. I'm scum.

 NEW ANSWER: I'd never do what this person is doing right now. I am better than this person at this moment in time.

5. What should I do instead of feel scared? Nothing, be nice and run away.

 NEW ANSWER: Ask a question to determine what is happening.

STEP 4: *Ask questions directly.*

Okay, here you go. The first chance you get, ask a significant other why he or she says or does something. Right now, go into your son, daughter, spouse or intimate's room and ask "Why did you say that to me a moment ago?" Spit the words out. If it was what he did rather than what he said to you, say "Why did you do that to me?" Phrase your question so that you ask about what you saw or heard. Be careful not to answer the question when you ask it. That happens when you ask, "Why are you angry at me?"

But do you *know* if the person is angry at you? Really? No, you don't know and you're not going to invite the person to say he or she is angry at you. Give no opportunities for people to blame you. Just ask the question in a straight-forward way: "Why did you do that?" or "Why did you say that?"

STEP 5: *Resist anxiety relief.*

You did it. You actually got the question out of your mouth. Okay, take a breather. That's one giant step for your future.

Now, stay where you are. Don't move, don't go backwards. It's not the end of the world. And for heaven's sake, *don't be fooled by your inner messages*. Inside your body is sending you distress signals warning you to "abort operation" and make amends before things get out of hand. You're itching to say, "Look, I'm sorry for asking you that silly question. Please forgive me." You feel the words form in your throat. Now they're on the tip of your tongue—HOLD IT!

Don't say you're sorry. Don't say you're sorry, because you're *not* sorry. You did nothing wrong. No facts, no fault—*F & F*. You must resist the rising anxiety that scares you into your old habits. Anxiety is when your body gets tense, you feel your thoughts spinning, your hands get sweaty, and you think OH NO, I'M IN DEEP SH__.

No, you're not. You can resist old habits by not rushing to relieve anxiety. It's okay to be a little bit anxious. That's normal. It doesn't mean you'll faint. Stay alert. Here are the wrong things to do. Don't do these things and you won't get more nervous.

- *Don't* say you're sorry.
- *Don't* defend yourself.
- *Don't* start complimenting the other person.
- *Don't* put yourself down.
- *Don't* give excuses.
- *Don't* blame somebody else.
- *Don't* cry.
- *Don't* do something nice for the other person.
- *Don't* laugh nervously.
- *Don't* change the subject.
- *Don't* remain silent.

There is nothing shameful about asking questions. Questions feel strange because you're afraid the person will tell you precisely what you fear—that you really are a bad person. But it's better for you to learn the facts first, than to conjure them up on your own. You will always distort the details if you make assumptions.

Roadblocks to Look Out For

You've taken the plunge off the cliff and never thought you'd make it safely to the bottom. Well, you have. You can ask questions about the way things are, not how you think they are. You can block automatic assumptions before they tongue-tie you into fear. This makes you feel stronger and more in control, and more comfortable.

Questions feel funny at first, but you will get over their strangeness. Other people, however, may take longer to get used to your questions. Think for a moment: How long have you been making assumptions? Your whole life? That means people who live with you know you by your habits. They are accustomed to having you tiptoeing around them, feeling guilty all the time, and especially, not asking them questions. They flip if you ask them a question. They don't know how to react, or what to say. So, they say what naturally enters their mind—and usually it's not very nice.

First time reactions to your questions can be negative. "What did you say to me?" or "Who do you think you're talking to?" raise the lid on your escape hatch—ready for ejection. You hate thinking you caused somebody grief and this is precisely what you may have done. Right?

Not exactly. You did catch him off guard. He's not sure which way to go—left, right or right down the center. So he punts. One way is by throwing you for a loop with nasty remarks, called *roadblocks*. Roadblocks are not intentional. Few people actually stay up nights to rehearse undermining tactics. It just comes naturally as a defense against looking stupid. Your questions instantly put him on the defensive because he lacks a response. You've never done this before and so he never needed to respond to you before. Now he does, and he doesn't know what to do.

Several roadblocks fly through the air as attempts to restore a comfort zone. Comfort zones for other people are having you be your polite, guilty self again. Drop your courage, get on your knees and beg forgiveness and they'll stop throwing roadblocks. But you have no intention of going backward. It was a long haul getting you this far and you're on a hot streak now. No turning back. That means bulldozing through roadblocks by handling them the right way. So, get used to hearing the following remarks after you ask questions, and learn to reply to them in a certain way.

ROADBLOCK: "Why are you asking me that question? Don't ask me that!"

ANSWER: "I'm just wondering."

ROADBLOCK: "You wonder too much. Keep your thoughts to yourself."

ANSWER: "I'm sorry you feel that way"

When people get huffy about your questions, use the conventional reply, "I'm just wondering" or "I'm sorry you feel that way." It instantly defuses defensive anger and makes the person feel silly for being rude. You, on the other hand, remain calm and collected. Take a breath, relax, and look at who is really getting nervous. It's not you—it's the other person. That person is so dizzy from your unexpected question that her remarks are running in circles. Nothing makes sense to her. She lost control for a moment. And you picked up control you never had before.

You're in charge, but a larger battalion of roadblocks is on its way. Roadblocks get nastier if the person literally has been verbally or physically abusive to you in the past. The person who always criticizes you, hits you, or has an emotional or substance abuse problem will get rougher in spite of your civil remarks. Their roadblocks get more interesting, but are treated the same way. Here are some common examples of roadblocks and how you can react to them.

ROADBLOCK: "There you go sticking your nose in other people's business."

Why they say it: This person is turning the topic around to avoid feeling stupid.

ANSWER: "That's not the point. I was just wondering."

ROADBLOCK: "You're never satisfied with anything I do—God you're awful."

Why they say it: This person is re-interpreting the topic and going way beyond the key points.

ANSWER: "I'm sorry you feel that way. But I was just wondering."

ROADBLOCK: "Listen, damn it, you ask me one more damn time and I'll show you who's boss here."

Why they say it: This person is threatening you with physical harm knowing that in the past this would shut you up immediately.

ANSWER: "I'm sorry you feel that way. I'm just wondering."

ROADBLOCK: "Boy do you look cute when you're pissed"

Why they say it: Belittling you with humor eases the person's tension.

ANSWER: "That's not the point. The point is (repeat your question)."

ROADBLOCK: "God, did I hurt your feelings? I'm such a horrible person. Don't look at me, I'm so stupid. "

Why they say it: Self-demeaning remarks in the past drew your sympathy.

ANSWER: "I'm sorry you feel that way." (Repeat your question).

ROADBLOCK: (Yelling loudly) "Shut the _____ up."

Why they say it: Aggressively loud threats in the past stopped you dead in your tracks. The person is hoping it will do the same thing again.

ANSWER: "I'm just wondering." (Repeat your question.)

ROADBLOCK: "You keep this up, you lousy skunk, and I'll tell the kids (or your family) what a jerk you really are."

Why they say it: Person threatens to expose your "weak" side hoping your need for approval will stop your questions.

ANSWER: "I'm sorry you feel that way." (Repeat question.)

Roadblocks set out in front of your soft ego are tie breakers. If the score is even, and you're holding up but feeling nervous, you may collapse under tougher criticisms. The more *personal* criticisms are, the more you feel compelled to react defensively. "How dare that person insult me that way!" But don't do that. Defensiveness gets you off track. You lose the link between F & F and asking questions. You'd plummet backward into old habits while the other person breathes a sigh of relief for escaping an uncomfortable situation. And that's precisely what you don't want to happen. You *want* that person to experience discomfort until he or she realizes you're really serious and won't give up.

Reversal of guilt

In spite of all this, a roadblock can also have a positive side—*if* it helps you reverse guilt. To do this, start by asking questions when you're:

- not sure why the person is asking or telling you something
- about to be accused of something you did or didn't do
- out of facts and need more information before replying intelligently

Questions transfer the weight of shame from your shoulders to the other person's shoulders long enough to hear more facts about what's going on. Replies they give when you reverse guilt are surprising. You may learn it's not your fault after all. Or, something entirely different is going on. For example, Cheryl heard her husband in the garage swearing up a storm and throwing his tools. She automatically assumed she misplaced his tools. But she reversed this guilt by going into the garage and asking him for facts: "Why are you yelling?" He replied that his brother borrowed his tool yesterday and forgot to return it. Plus, he was tired and felt a cold coming on. *It had nothing to do with Cheryl.*

By reversing the burden of shame, you force a person to explain what's going on in the situation. You can resist blaming yourself for things you didn't do but think you did. You can resist rescuing the situation from conflict and making the person feel like a happy camper. You don't step in and hurt yourself or repair something because you *won't do that without your facts.* Your facts are the life-blood of your social interaction. Think only facts. Look only at facts. Talk only facts. And suspend the verdict of guilty on yourself or others until all the facts are lined up for discussion.

STEP 4:
No More Avoidance and Escape

Do you know how bad it feels being stuck in the house when you're sick? Do you know how confined you feel when it's raining outside and you must stay indoors? Well, try multiplying that feeling times a thousand. You're not confined, you're *trapped*. You're a victim. You have nowhere to go; you're held prisoner in your own home or around people you don't want to be around. You hate being there; you hate being with them. You can't stand it. You want out. But you're stuck forever—or are you?

No, not if you use avoidance behavior. You *avoid* things you really don't want to deal with or can't deal with. For example, conflict; you hate conflict. Fear of its happening triggers you to do something—to prevent, delay or stop the conflict. The harder you try, the harder your heart beats. Anxiety rises, followed by sweaty palms, tight shoulders and dizziness. Inside you feel like a steam engine. You panic. *What if I can't avoid this situation or this person? What if it happens? What if nothing I say or do delays or stops bad things from happening?* Easy. You'll feel guilty.

Avoidance is your natural defense against guilt. You sink into frightening situations you're bound to feel ashamed about. Fear devours your commonsense. You lose all sense of space and time, and completely obsess over preventive action. "How can I stop conflict from happening?" "How can I do it now?" Concentration is deep. You think rapidly and strategically of detours to fool the people around you. *They must not know what I'm doing, so I must do it right and act fast.* It feels like a combat zone. It's you against the enemy. Your mission is avoiding the

39

opposition. And if you lose, you lose big. So keep your eyes open, your body alert, and be ready to sprint when your internal fear-alarm goes off.

The problem is that it always goes off. Nearly everything triggers your fear-alarm because there is much in the world you wish to avoid. That's why this step is very important. It's the step showing you simple solutions to fight the urge to avoid unpleasant situations. Fear prevents you from entering bad situations or getting out of (escaping) them as soon as possible. Even if you feel brave, that urge is tough to beat. *Fear always overrides logic.* But, you can demolish fear and stick-it-out if you realize exactly what your avoidance and escape behaviors are, and what you can do differently in the future.

What Is Avoidance and Escape?

Again, consider what avoidance and escape mean.

AVOIDANCE: When you go through certain words and actions to delay, prevent, or stop something from happening.

ESCAPE: When you're already caught in the unwanted situation and try like the dickens to get out of that situation.

Your life is full of avoidance and escape situations. Many are obvious—like avoiding arguments. Many are routine—like avoiding sex or doing things for yourself. And many are subtle—like keeping your pencils lined up in a straight row, or repeatedly saying "I'm sorry." Here are more situations you might identify with. Go ahead and check off which ones fit you like a glove.

_____ 1. Not going to bed until your spouse comes to bed

_____ 2. Not eating until all others finish eating

_____ 3. Not talking until others start the conversation

_____ 4. Not offering your opinion

_____ 5. Not walking ahead of the crowd

_____ 6. Not arriving somewhere first

_____ 7. Not saying *no*

_____ 8. Not talking about problems in front of the kids

_____ 9. Not doing things for yourself

_____ 10. Not trying new foods, new restaurants or new stores

_____ 11. Not sounding smart

_____ 12. Not looking at people when they look at you

_____ 13. Not sounding sad when you're feeling sad

_____ 14. Not saying you're angry

Now you add some. Jot down two or three examples of what you avoid or who you avoid. Do you avoid people? Do you avoid situations?

PEOPLE
- I avoid (name) _____, because (reason) _____.
- I avoid (name) _____, because (reason) _____.
- I avoid (name) _____, because (reason) _____.

SITUATIONS
- I avoid (situation) _____, because it (reason) _____.
- I avoid (situation) _____, because it (reason) _____.
- I avoid (situation) _____, because it (reason) _____.

Why you avoid is another story. There are many reasons, some obvious and some subtle. Obvious reasons include recent events that make you feel upset and terribly guilty. Being told *you're stupid* two days ago is still fresh in your mind. You still feel angry about it today, and absolutely don't want to be anywhere near that critic. Subtle reasons are too distant to pinpoint a specific cause, although pieces of the puzzle are easy to figure out. Suppose it wasn't two days ago. Maybe nobody has criticized you in awhile. But the moment you walk into, say, a clothing store, *something hits you like a lightning bolt.* You feel it instantly. Cold shivers run up and down your spine, leaving you bewildered and almost paralyzed. You can't move or think straight. All you want to do is *get out of there fast.*

Reflecting for a moment, you realize the interior of that store reminds you of a clothing store where you and your mother went shopping when you were a child. She made you hate that store. Everything you tried on didn't fit. You knew it, and she *made* you know it. You felt fat and ugly, and you even remember the salespeople laughing at you behind the counter. The horrible experience you suffered at the store made a painful impression. You hated that store. You never went into it again. Soon it went out of business and your memories faded along with it. That is, until you were struck by similar impressions going into this other store.

Another subtle reason you may avoid or escape may have nothing to do with people or situations. It has to do with how you feel inside. Sensations vary from nervous tension to aches and pains, to feeling warm, cold, elated, depressed and in between. You go through normal physical cycles as the day wears on. Internally your body sensations fluctuate all the time; stable body temperature and stable feelings are impossible. But problems arise if you feel one sensation that triggers fear. For instance, think back to your childhood when your parents argued. Was it at night? Was it during the day? If it was at night, how did you feel—physically—as you listened? Were you tired? Let's suppose you were tired.

As an adult, you also get tired in the evening. As the evening wears on, you may also notice an acute need to *stay away from people.* You withdraw from your children, spouse, or friends and feel okay about it. Distance puts you safely away from any chance of conflict. Conflict may never have occurred, but you naturally feel the urge to pull away because sleepiness signals *something bad might happen, just as it did years ago in your childhood.*

Physical sensations, like situations and people, trigger the urge for avoidance and escape in different ways. Here are major styles of avoidance you probably display in one way or another.

Different types of avoidance and escape
Take steps ahead of conflict. You may sense a conflict is brewing. You don't know for sure, but there's no time to waste. Preliminary maneuvers are put into action in anticipation of a problem so that you can nip it in the bud. You may apologize, re-arrange a schedule, make personal sacrifices, yell, scream, or do just about anything to *buy time.* That's all you want. Just

enough time to defuse and dismantle the ticking time bomb you absolutely believe will explode in minutes.

No curiosity in trying new things. You *never* want to make a fool of yourself no matter how simple the new situation is. New situations that are outside of your comfort zone—that is, that zone where you know everything and everybody—are avoided like the plague. When you try new things, you risk looking stupid, incompetent, and childish. When you pride yourself on staying within the comfort zone, even curiosity is squelched, and alternative behaviors are left untried. In that zone you feel in control. Watching people laugh or do outrageous and goofy things means *they are out of control.* You refuse to be out of control, so you forfeit thinking about or actually trying new behaviors.

Staying quiet. The less said, the less exposed. Again, *protect yourself from looking stupid.* Avoidance commonly takes the form of saying nothing in social situations. You may enter a situation quietly or suddenly decide to be quiet after feeling intimidated by things going on. That's an example of escape behavior. Silence gets you out of *potential trouble.* You don't know what that trouble may be, or who may cause that trouble, but you never-the-less feel trouble rising on the horizon.

Always giving excuses. "I don't want to do this because..." is your reflex answer. It just comes out of your mouth. It happens every time you feel scared or ashamed, or any time you anticipate trouble. You immediately escape the situation by inventing some believable reason and qualifying it with all sorts of reasons until you get your way. Your reasons may be true, may be false, but they're still excuses.

Aggression. "Anger scares him away." Getting angry stops a person dead in his tracks. They don't expect you to raise your voice or use foul language. They don't expect you to challenge them or be defensive. So, when you do these things, it's shocking. They don't know how to react. That stops the conflict right away.

Of course, that's the wrong way to stop conflict. You're using anger before conflict happens to make sure *it doesn't happen*. And you're using anger immediately after conflict begins *to escape* conflict before it gets worse.

Crying. Sometimes the person stopped dead in their tracks is you. You just freeze up. You're completely numb. Conflict, criticism and rejection put a straight jacket on you. You don't move. You say nothing. You do nothing. You feel that anything you might say or do will be wrong. You want to hide, but you can't. You can't get away. You're stuck there. That's when you cry. Crying *avoids* more conflict by making the person feel sorry for you.

And sometimes crying backfires. Tears trigger predators to get more angry, more violent, more verbally abusive, or more neglectful. You cry harder, but that makes attacks more vicious. So, why do you keep crying? Is it a matter of survival? Yes. That's all you know how to do. You don't know how to fight. You don't know how to run away. And you're terrified of saying or doing anything else.

Distrusting everything and everybody. Doing everything yourself is a sure-fire way of avoiding two things. One is relying on people. Second is owing people obligations. You can't trust people enough to say, "Will you do this for me?" They may do it wrong. They probably won't do it perfectly. And you'll do it better and faster. You also hate imposing on people to do something for you. They'll perceive you as "selfish" and "pushy."

Relying on people also creates an obligation. And you hate obligations. Obligations means you *owe* people favors. You feel you *must* do this or that for them when they want it. You're at the mercy of their time schedule, their needs and their *control*. Owing people makes you feel like a prisoner being interrogated. No matter what you say or do you're wrong. You're damned if you do and damned if you don't. Not repaying the favor means you're derelict and that will make you feel guilty. But repaying the favor you owe somebody may fall below their expectations. You may not have done enough for them. That also makes you feel guilty. One way or another you get sucked into shame. It's a no-win situation.

Poor concentration. When you feel emotionally paralyzed, all mental circuits get blocked. You can't concentrate on what somebody is saying or doing. All you keep thinking about is *why you're a bad person, what you did wrong, and how you must avoid or escape the situation.* Concentration lapses in any situation where fear strikes and you don't have a clue as to how to deal with the fear.

Procrastination. You dread doing something. It doesn't matter who it's for—you or somebody else. You literally drag yourself to get the task started. Finally, once you get into it, two things happen. Either you start and stop the task and delay it further and further. Or, you can't stop doing it. You go into a frenzy. All mental focus is upon doing this task. Nothing can interrupt you. Your entire body is wired to the task from beginning to end.

Procrastination occurs for three reasons. First, you avoid starting something you honestly believe you can't do or can't do well. No matter how hard you try, it just won't come out satisfactorily. So, you put it off until the very end.

A second reason for procrastination is that you hate starting anything new or tedious. Tedious labor feels overwhelming and frustrating. You can't figure out what to do first. You're not sure of priorities. You're not sure the task is even necessary. Anger rises when you push yourself into difficult tasks only to discover obstacles at every turn. So, you make an ambitious start and then stop as soon as pressure builds up. Pressure is the feeling that *you don't know how to do this because you are stupid and lazy.*

A third reason is habit. You've grown accustomed, over many years, to waiting until the very last second to do things. You're an eleventh-hour person. When the final bell rings, you're amazingly efficient. Days can go by without laying a hand on the task. You put it off knowing that shortly before time runs out you will buckle down and get the job done. Suppose, for example, you've been asked to make two pumpkin pies for Thanksgiving. Come Wednesday night, at eleven PM, you're rushing through the kitchen in a frenzy baking the pies. And, sure enough, you get them done.

Planning ahead *does occur to you*, but you ignore those thoughts. In fact, you strive to plan ahead. But every time you try doing things ahead of schedule it backfires. You feel there's too much time wasted between doing the task and when the task is due. You feel bored, apathetic, and down on yourself for being lazy. Instead, you stuff your planning hours with all sorts of other *competing* tasks to feel busy. That way when you make those pies at the last minute you lie to yourself by saying, "Gee, it's the first time all week I've had time to do this."

Hypersensitive to criticism. Nobody likes criticism. But criticism to you is like a syringe. It digs deeply into your most sensitive vein causing intense self-criticism and resentment. You instantly feel angry at yourself for being too vulnerable and letting the other person catch you off guard. You even agree with what the person accused you of: *It has to be true, it always is.* Then, after shaming yourself, you react violently inside, feeling an intense need to retaliate against the accuser. You can't express your feelings aloud. That's out of the question: it's too scary. So you conspire secretly to take revenge, somehow hurting the accuser behind his or her back. That way you think the person will *know* how you felt and will never criticize you again.

But it doesn't work. In fact, revenge always backfires. Hiding things, forgetting to tell people things, ruining things, and simply not doing what you're asked feels for the moment like you've inconvenienced the accuser and taught that person a lifelong lesson. But the only lesson they've learned is to get angrier, more cynical, and more critical of you.

Deeply absorbed in people's feelings. Seeing people upset is contagious. You feel their emotions just as if you were suffering those exact emotions yourself. It feels identical. They cry—you cry. They hurt—you hurt. What goes through them goes through you. And it doesn't matter who the person is. Television characters, neighbors, friends, and relatives all make you feel that way.

You become absorbed in people's feeling for three reasons. First, it helps you escape feeling guilty for their bad feelings. You can't stand, for example, seeing anyone cry. You immediately blame yourself: *God, what did I do to cause this person to cry?* or *God, how can I let this person cry?* You either feel guilty for *causing* the crying or *not stopping* the crying. Either way, the blame is on you. You relieve this self-shame by doing something for the person. You may step forward and help the person directly, or you may just *feel* for them. That way you stop hurting inside, and you can say you *tried* making the person feel better.

A second reason you get engulfed in other people's feelings is to avoid conflict, criticism or rejection. People in distress *need you*. Feeling needed puts you in a dilemma. If you ignore the person, you may get reprimanded. The person may say bad things about you or hate you. If you help the person, surely that will prevent disapproval and rejection. Impulsively, you rescue the distressed person to avoid immediate and future repercussions.

The last reason is most "catchy." Automatically, you drift to suffering people because you love to help others. Relieving their suffering brings you happiness. You live off their pride. How much they recover determines how effective you are. How happy they are determines how happy you are. You feel good when you see them back on their feet and self-confident.

However, you're actually living through others. They've become your life-support system, without which you feel empty, useless and helpless. You're like a Christmas ornament that only shines when it is pinned onto the Christmas tree—alone it's dull. By living people's emotions you avoid your own self-hate and self-shame feelings. You believe that saving other people from misery earns you a reason for feeling important.

However, this backfires. You actually get the short end of the deal. What really occurs is that you end up rescuing the same people from the same problems time and time again. These people never learn how to rescue themselves. They like having you do it. And so you become their lifeline forever.

Discrediting everything you do. You hate looking selfish. Doing anything for yourself feels wrong. The same is true of what you say. Opinions, disagreements, even spontaneous comments all risk sounding arrogant. And arrogance pushes people away, when what you want is to bring them closer to you. Sure, you try editing your words, phrases, even thinking hours ahead of time about the right actions to prevent disapproval. But "mental" rehearsals can't prevent unexpected reactions. That's when you turn to discrediting everything you do.

Anytime your words or actions seem slightly better than somebody else, or somewhat impressive, you disqualify their value instantly before you get criticized or alienated. You can't bear hearing somebody accuse you of being pig-headed, of "tooting your own horn," or having people think you're a braggart. Hearing them say this about you makes you feel ashamed. You're ashamed of feeling important. *Importance* is reserved for really great triumphs like winning the lottery, earning a degree, or rescuing somebody from a burning house. Those things deserve recognition. Right?

Wrong. Even if you jumped out of a moving vehicle to rescue a helpless dog in the middle of traffic, you still wouldn't allow yourself the credit. You would say the action was something anybody would do in the same situation. And there's no reason for you to think you're somebody special. You attribute all of your actions to routine, garden-variety tasks that everybody does, no matter how risky the act or successful the outcome.

Solving Avoidance and Escape

That's what you do now. But not anymore. Now you know what avoidance and escape are. Now you can pinpoint how they sneak into your thoughts and actions—how they become all consuming. Avoidance and escape have trapped you long enough. So, here's what to do: *Set up opportunities for conflict, watch out for the wrong type of conflict opportunities, and use a special assertiveness approach.*

Set up opportunities for conflict

Giving opinions. It's time to exercise your vocal chords. Giving your opinion means you'll risk conflict and lots of other nasty things. But not if you're prepared and know what you're doing. Follow these steps to test giving your opinion.

1. Choose somebody you know—even your significant other. It should be an adult.

2. Listen to something they say.

3. Make a comment about what they say. Your comment adds to their statement. For example, if the person says, "It's cold outside today." Say, "Yah, it's supposed to get down to thirty degrees by nightfall."

4. Do not just agree with the person.

5. Do not just nod your head or make grunting sounds.

A second way to give opinions is to initiate the comment. Do this:

1. Choose a person you know or your significant other.

2. Strike up a conversation about something neutral. It should not be a topic the person likes to talk about or that will flatter the person.

Disagreements. Take opinions to the next step by saying something different or opposite to what the person you're talking to says. That's a disagreement. You're accustomed to remaining silent or getting angry when opposing thoughts enter your mind. Now you'll break out of that mold.

DO:

1. Choose a person you know or your significant other.

2. Listen to what the person is saying.

3. Immediately say what you're thinking. If you think, "That's wrong," say "That's wrong." If you think, "That doesn't make sense," say "That doesn't make sense." Let out your spontaneous thoughts and feelings. No holding back. Say it when you feel it and think it.

4. Handle angry replies by saying, "Well, that's just my opinion" or "I'm sorry you feel that way."

DO NOT:

1. Say "I'm sorry."
2. Defend your disagreement.
3. Disqualify your remarks before making them (e.g., "I don't know much about this, but ...").
4. Discredit your remarks after making them (e.g., "I'm probably wrong about what I said ...").
5. Blame the other person for not liking your disagreement.

Criticism of another. Opinions and disagreements get your foot in the door. But to open the door wider you need to take higher risks. It's time to close your eyes and try something you honestly feel is suicide. Believe me, it's not; it just feels that way. Try to criticize another person. Here's how:

1. Choose somebody you know or your significant other.
2. Find some fault with that person, and tell him about it.
3. Make the statement once, without repeating it, dragging it out or beating it to death. One statement will do fine. For example, you might say, "Your fingernails are awfully dirty."
4. Let the person respond. If the response is negative, just say "I'm sorry you feel that way." DO NOT REPEAT YOURSELF. If it is positive, say "I'm glad you agree with me." LET IT GO AT THAT.

A funny thing happens once you try this out and see that it works okay. You suddenly feel the urge to discuss everything bad that ever happened to you. In fact, once you start blaming, it becomes *complaining.* You feel that it's hunting season on anything and anybody who ever wronged you. But that's a mistake. Just keep your focus on one criticism at a time.

Defiance and taboo. Now be a little more daring. Do things against the family or household code of "right and wrong." This code is not an ethical or moral code. Violating the code does not make you evil. Instead, most rules that develop between parents and children, spouses and family members come from unspoken agreements. For instance, "Don't tell people we yell at the kids." or "Never tell anybody your spouse is verbally or physically abusive toward you." Such rules develop to protect you, your significant other or family from outside scrutiny. You don't want others thinking badly of you and causing you guilt. So you censor certain events.

Now is your time to lift the censorship. It's time to spread the news by saying and doing things that seem taboo, or dangerously wicked and rebellious. Let out your frustrations by stepping over that secret boundary.

1. Identify one family taboo or "no-no." For example, your friends should not call after a certain time at night.

2. Set in motion ways to violate this taboo. For example, tell one or two friends to call late in the evening.

3. When the taboo is broken, get ready for conflict. Somebody will be upset that you broke the taboo. That's okay. It's natural, and must occur so that you can learn how to handle it.

You must inconvenience or annoy another person to make changes. Keeping people happy never changes a situation.

4. When the person reacts negatively, just say, "I'm sorry you feel that way."

5. Do not agree to "talk about it" at once. Wait until another day and for the person to cool down.

6. Do not repent by apologizing, feeling guilty, or doing nice things for the person so he or she will be happy with you.

Saying no. You've already spoken up, disagreed with someone, criticized something, and rubbed someone the wrong way by breaking sacred house rules. It's beginning to feel good. But you're still very scared. You think you're pushing your luck. How much more will it take before the dam will burst? One more thing? Is it already too late? No. Not at all. You've only just begun.

Now you're ready to say *no*. Saying *no* is to blatantly refuse requests, routines, and expectations from friends and family. You're not committed to do everything that everybody wants you to do no matter what they say or how you feel inside. Your intuition may say "Nonsense, you better do these things ... or else." But that's so you can avoid and escape feeling guilty. Don't listen to your intuition. It's wrong. Listen instead to your internal voice that begs you to try new things. Try this:

1. Choose a person you know or your significant other.

2. When that person asks you to do something that you always do, say *no*. Routine things are the best target for refusal. Refuse to drive the kids one day. Refuse to go grocery shopping. Refuse to take things to the cleaners. Refuse to go to work. Refuse to make a meal. Refuse to do something you routinely do to assist someone else.

3. When you say *no,* do something for yourself instead. For example, refuse to mow the lawn; sunbathe in the back yard, instead. This will feel very wrong and taboo. That's how you know you're doing it right! You're entitled to be selfish once in a while. Son't be scared. Just try it.

4. If people react negatively, just say "I'm sorry you feel this way, but you'll have to come up with an alternative." Do not help the person brainstorm a solution to relieve your guilty feelings for causing them an inconvenience. This is not the time or place to work on problem solving skills. You'll work on that later. This is the time to say *no* and let the other person adjust.

Selfishness. Is there a way to be bold without overdoing it? Sure there is. But it takes a little nerve. You've already violated household taboos and said *no* when your intuition pleaded for you to say *yes*. How about stretching your lucky streak a bit longer? You can be selfish by choosing to do personal things you frequently ignore, dismiss or think are wrong. You've always wanted to do them but have felt ashamed. Now you can indulge in your personal wants with some moderation. Here's how:

1. Announce to a friend or significant other that you plan to spend a moderate amount of money, time or energy buying or doing something for yourself. You may wish to buy some clothing or just go shopping. You may wish to attend a sporting event or watch it on TV. You may want to eat at a special restaurant. Or, even simpler, just take time off from work. The choice remains up to you.

2. Handle the other person's resistance by saying, "I'm sorry you feel that way, but this is my plan." Do not make excuses for sounding too rough or selfish about your needs. You deserve personal time and you don't owe anybody an apology for doing what should be natural.

3. Be sure to follow through on your promise. If you say you're doing ABC, make sure you do ABC. Follow through convinces others you are serious. Make your *I-want* messages sound strong and reliable so that in the future you'll encounter less resistance and more cooperation.

Close-in body space. Just verbalizing *I-want* messages is half the battle. The other half involves physically stepping in to the person's *space* when you talk to him. Invading someone else's space instantly gives force to your words and body language. You come across confidently, assertively, and able to defuse angry reactions. Try moving closer to the person by doing five things:

1. Before you speak, walk up to the chosen person or significant other.

2. Look directly into that person's eyes and then speak.

3. Stay in close proximity until all your words are out.

4. Even as mini-conflict starts, stay right there and say your "I'm sorry you feel that way" or something similar.

5. Walk away after you've had your say.

Demand reciprocity. "I'll scratch your back if you'll scratch mine." It's not a cute saying—it's the *law*. Make sure your efforts get rewarded. Put a price tag on all generous gestures. Sure, you'll help out. You'll drive the kids to dance class, *but only if everybody else takes a turn.* Favors you do must always be returned with a favor, if not that day then very soon afterwards.

Asking people to return favors may feel like an imposition. You feel they will misjudge you as calculating and manipulative. They'll think you're a greedy person, only looking out for yourself. Thinking this way has tricked you into saying *yes* too many times without benefits in return. But you can stop this one-way assistance.

1. When asked to do something for another person, immediately ask them to do something for you. Don't wait until you need a favor. The more you let time pass, the less incentive the person has to do you a favor. Reciprocal favors must be seized upon when the other person *needs you to do something now.* Make the price of your helpfulness be their efforts.

2. Vague promises such as "Well, sure, I'll do this for you later," are no good. Promises hold little water. You want rapid action. They should be willing to help you out as quickly and efficiently as you help them out. Let it always be a two-way street. One-way helping is unacceptable.

3. Tell the person precisely what you want. Your request should be realistic, simple, small, within the person's ability, and require about the same time and effort as what you're doing for the person. For example, you'll pick up coffee for them while you're at the grocery store if they'll keep an eye on your kids while you're gone.

Your efforts are not free. You've been giving them away for a long time without daring to ask for anything in return. Now you're asking for more than *thanks.* You're insisting that they pay the piper.

Interrupt a task. Getting into a task is difficult. Either you delay it until the very last moment, or you dive in head first and deeply immerse yourself in it without coming up for air. Staying deeply enmeshed in a task helps prevent your feeling guilty for not doing it earlier. A side-effect of this indulgence is refusing to interrupt yourself once you get started.

Try interrupting the task you're deeply wired into by doing the following:

1. Divide the task period into small time intervals. Rest after each interval. For instance, an hour (60 minutes) job breaks down into three 20-minute periods.

2. After 20 minutes, you put down the tools, stand up or leave the room, and go to a rest area. Rest areas consist of any relaxing, nontask situation, from visiting with kids to talking on the telephone. Nontasks last for 5 to 10 minutes, never leading to a new task or becoming a permanent distraction from the task at hand.

3. Return to the task at hand for another 20-minute period.

A second way of interrupting the task is asking somebody to deliberately call your attention away from what you're doing when you're not expecting it.

1. Ask a spouse, the children or peers to "bother you" at odd times during your on-task work time.

2. Immediately put down your things and attend to the other person. You're not stopping your task to make other people feel good. You're doing it so that you can interrupt an obsessive-compulsive work pace.

3. Interruptions may still put you on the defensive although choreographed ahead of time. That requires you to use the relaxation methods discussed in the next chapter.

Wrong types of conflict opportunities

While practicing these new steps, old habits may sneak back in because they feel comfortable and you may mistake *comfort* for feeling *in control.* It happens all the time. Even when you think you've taken every precaution. Even if you have a tremendous desire to be a different person. Somehow, some way, old habits play bad tricks on you. That's why it pays to be on top of common DON'Ts for setting up conflict opportunities. No matter how easy it is, familiar it is, or right it seems, do not do the following things.

DON'T: Do things behind the person's back.

Here's why: Secretly seeking justice for feeling guilty, or emotionally helpless, only spurs the person to continue hurting you. Your actions are indirect and create more bad-will and unfounded inferences as to why you sneaked behind their back to do something. This infuriates the person causing him or her to retaliate with greater intensity.

INSTEAD: Be upfront and ask questions. Then tell the person why you are upset about what happened. Never fear being direct. A direct person is a confident person. And that confidence eliminates feelings of shame.

DON'T: Retaliate for the sake of getting even.

Here's why: Proving you're right by equaling the score sends a clear message that now it's the other person's move. It's in his corner now. You may feel retaliation stops guilt and restores feelings of control, but this feeling is fake. It's the wrong type of control: unhealthy control. Healthy control is asserting your views, taking your lumps, and learning to walk away from a fight even if you feel you are right or can win it.

INSTEAD: Be flexible. Just say NBD—No Big Deal. Who cares if the person "gotcha." So what? Does it really spoil your week? Does it really undermine your integrity? Are you really the laughing stock of your friends? Probably not. Only you can end your embarrassment by letting this situation go.

You're probably saying, "But that's what I always do. I always turn away and say it doesn't matter. That's when I get burned." True, you get burned by saying nothing and hoping conflict will go away. So you're thinking that doing the opposite—getting revenge—will change your passive style. Not so. There's a better way to react. It deals with being assertive in a way we'll see in a few minutes.

DON'T: Get as tough as the other person.

Here's why: Proving you're strong, powerful, or untouchable detaches you from all emotion. You feel that anger. The angrier you get, the more compelling your arguments. You also think that anger might scare off the mean person. A show of strength is pure avoidance behavior; you're avoiding conflict by meeting muscle with muscle, and skipping over words, ideas and good communication.

INSTEAD: Choose what you want to say and say it. Be brief, but be direct. Keep your aggressive muscle tucked away. Don't let it out. It accomplishes nothing.

DON'T: Withdraw to a hiding place.

Here's why: You sense defeat and figure you must minimize your losses by retreating quickly to a safe place before being taken prisoner. The enemy is whoever is angry with you. You hide for safety and think the conflict will go away. But conflict never goes away. It just dematerializes for the moment and re-materializes in another form at another time. Your efforts to hide are in vain.

INSTEAD: Figure out what the problem is and ask questions about it. Face it head on knowing you're going to feel hurt, guilty or anxious. Expect to feel these things. No amount of dodging the inevitable pains of confrontation can ease the way.

DON'T: Smoke cigarettes, drink alcohol, or use other drugs

Here's why: Does a joint a day keep the anger away? Of course not—but it's hard to tell that to your body. Smoking cigarettes, popping pills, drinking alcohol or using other drugs instantly shifts you into avoidance land. You escape frustration; you escape conflict, criticism and rejection; and you escape your shame. Substances give temporary relief from major life problems instead of facing those problems head on.

INSTEAD: If you're using any substance, realize why you're using it. It either slows you down or speeds you up. Either direction artificially creates peace and quiet. A peace and quiet that ends just as quickly as it begins. So, stop running away through excessive use of cigarettes, coffee, alcohol, drugs, sex, or other addictive behaviors. Interrupt the cycle by first looking at what starts the substance use cycle. Then resist using the substance as long as you can. At first, resist until you feel especially nervous or afraid; that's your *emotional withdrawal*. Once you can get this far, you're ready to handle the trouble yourself, without a boost from these substances.

DON'T: Have an extramarital affair

Here's why: It's great to hear people say they want you, care for you, and really think you're special—especially when you've never heard these words before. Your parents never said it. Well, maybe once or twice. Your spouse never said it. Well, maybe once or twice. And your friends never say it. Not even once or twice. Suddenly you've met a person who listens to you! You don't have to do very much to please the person. *Everything you do pleases this person.* It's too amazing. It's unrealistic.

But it's true. You're suddenly feeling infatuated by another person who says and does everything you ever wanted from a loving partner. So, why can't you "go for it"? It's simple. You're married. Relationships outside of marriage never work. Maybe after the marriage ends they do, but during the marriage such a relationship forms as a "make-me-feel-good" substitute for the real thing. Such relationships compensate for what you don't get and what you don't know how to get. And worse than that: This perfect person who says and does everything your spouse doesn't say or do may have a bag of other problems you're not seeing right at the moment. Frequently those problems are exactly the things you hate in your marriage.

Extramarital relationships are bad news because they avoid and escape the real issue. They avoid dealing with communication and sexual problems. They provide escape from hurt feelings, abuse, and intense anxiety. Infidelity never solves these problems. But infidelity does create new problems. Now you must engage in more avoidance and escape behaviors to hide your lover and keep your rendezvous points secret. You must lie, cheat, and pull away physically from your spouse to establish loyalty to your lover. You must always look behind your back in case people you know see you. You become an undercover agent working an undercover romance.

INSTEAD: When loving friends want intimacy, immediately confront the obvious: WHY? Ask yourself, "I'm already using avoidance behaviors—do I really need more avoidance in my life?" Second, refuse intimacy and use the situation as a gauge of how vulnerable you are for compassion. It's time you confront your spouse on the topic.

DON'T: Quit your job

Here's why: "I'll show them who's the boss" can backfire real quickly. It leads to a long wait in the unemployment line. Avoiding stress, you'd think, involves leaving the job. But it doesn't. Leaving the job without trying to first solve job stresses is cutting your nose off to spite your face. You need your nose to breathe. And you need a job for independent income. That superior feeling of causing your employers or peers great inconvenience is temporary. They really don't care. They'll just replace you with another person. It's life as usual there. But your grief turns major. You have to scrounge around for another job, re-prove your credentials, and basically start all over. Part of another job may even entail dealing with similar employer-employee problems.

INSTEAD: Solve the problems once, at your current job, and you'll never feel helpless again at other jobs.

DESC assertiveness

Speaking up, saying *no* and expressing your anger all come under the heading of *assertiveness*. Usually assertiveness means "protecting your rights" or giving people a piece of your mind. The more they hear of your feelings, the better you relieve your feelings. And partly this is true. You do have a right to express your feelings. And you do relieve your bad feelings by releasing them aloud. But that's only the beginning.

Just having the *right* and *need* for self-expression might not stir your juices. It takes a lot more. It takes *risk*. What is the risk of saying the first thing that comes to your mind? Check off which ones apply to you.

_____ I'll sound stupid.

_____ I'll bother people.

_____ I'll regret it later.

_____ It won't matter anyway.

And even worse, if you act on instinct, talking before thinking, and it goes bad, what are you afraid might happen?

_____ I'll pay for it by being teased or criticized.

_____ People will hate me.

_____ I'll be down on myself for days.

Many "knee-jerk" reactions might occur. They always have, and there's no reason to think that today or tomorrow it will be any different. Except for one reason: Today you are trying new behaviors so you can handle all these knee-jerk reflexes. Preventing them would be nice, but it's unlikely. That's why the second best approach is confronting problems *after* they happen.

You've been too careful, too calculated about preventing bad things. And look what's happened. Bad things still occurred.

You can't prevent them, so you shouldn't be overly concerned with preventing conflict, criticism and rejection. Normal human interactions involve conflict, criticism and rejection. They're part of healthy living. Everyday, some person invariably will say or do something that will strike you the wrong way, no matter what you say or do. Count on it. But dealing with these problems once they occur is different. There you have control in changing behavior.

That's the point of **DESC**. DESC is an acronym. It stands for Describe, Express, Specify and Consequences. Each step follows a simple order for getting your message across to people who *offend you*. They offend you either by *what they say*, or *how they say it*. That is, by their words or actions. Words can be offensive for many reasons. The person is using profanity, being condescending, belittling you, or talking bad about loved ones. Actions speak louder than words only because you "read into" the actions. Silence can be offensive, so can rough and rigid gestures, a loud voice, or the person always crying.

Okay, but let's ask the obvious. If what or how they're saying something is so offensive, why don't they know it? "Why am I the only person who finds it offensive? What if what I find offensive *really is not offensive?*"

That's why you check out your facts. Never rely on guesses. Try using this standard to prove behavior is offensive.

Standard for determining offensive behavior

If the behavior makes you angry, is it (1) because of what was said, or (2) how the person said it?

These characteristics make it offensive. But if you say, "No, no, it's not what she said or how she said it, it's *why* she said it." That means the behavior may not be offensive. Offensive behavior is only what you *see* and *hear*. It is also what others see and hear. Reading beneath the surface or tapping hidden meanings you believe motivate the offensive action does not make the action offensive.

And here's the second problem. Suppose you know it's absolutely offensive behavior. Docs that mean the other person agrees her behavior is offensive? Probably not. The offender usually is oblivious to being offensive at the time. Even admitting it does not mean they can instantly change the behavior or accept responsibility for it. So, how can you make people own their offensive actions and relieve yourself of feeling guilty about it?

That's the purpose of DESC, and here's how to use it.

D = Describe

Describe means you are telling the offensive person exactly what he or she did or said made you angry. Spell it out in no uncertain terms.

WHAT TO SAY: "Bill, you just *yelled* at me."

E = Express

Express means you briefly tell how you felt about what the person said or did to you. Keep the words to a minimum.

WHAT TO SAY: "Bill, that hurt my feelings."

S = Specify

Specify means you tell the person what you want him to do instead of the offensive words or actions. You give alternatives. Alternatives must be simple to do, in understandable language, and doable right *now*. Never ask for a promise to do it later. Later doesn't count. What counts is right now.

This guide will help you figure out "alternative" behaviors. Ask the other person to:

- do the opposite of what he's doing
- clarify why he's doing it
- do something else positive
- do something positive that he already knows how to do.

WHAT TO SAY: "Bill, how about lowering your voice."

C = Consequences

It would be nice if that's all you had to do. Imagine the offensive person happily saying, "Gee, thanks for pointing out that behavior of mine. You're such a great person to do that." Wouldn't that be nice? Well, dream on.

It rarely happens that way. Usually, the offensive person is astounded you even opened your mouth, let alone asserted a flow of words challenging what he said. But that's what you did, and you're not about to back down from it. So, you must be prepared to use consequences for the person unwilling to hear you out.

What is a consequence? Do you threaten the person? "Hey, you better shut up or else!" No, that's wrong to do.

Do you deliver ultimatums that threaten to strip away all the other person's privileges, or threaten separation and divorce? No, that's also wrong.

Well, if those things don't work, what will work? "How can I hurt this person enough to get my point across?" That's the problem. You don't want to hurt or threaten to get good behavior. You get good behavior with *positive, not negative,* incentives. You dangle a carrot, not a shotgun, in front of the person's face for faster results.

Consequences are those carrots. Ask yourself "What does this person want from me at this very moment?" That is, why is she yelling at me? Why is he calling me names? The thing the person wants from you—usually your attention—is precisely the reward you offer when using the format for consequences. Don't hunt around for powerful rewards. Don't promise meals, sex, or other things you think the person wants just to get the behavior you want. Those rewards are fake and will not work. Use what the person wants from you. Be willing to give your attention, to listen, even to compromise on touchy subjects, all in return for the behavior changes you ask for.

WHAT TO SAY: "Bill, IF you lower your voice, THEN I'll listen to what you have to say. But, IF you keep on yelling, THEN I have got other things to do."

PUT IT TOGETHER: Here's how it works as one long string of sentences.

> "Bill, you just yelled at me."
> "That hurt my feelings."
> "How about lowering your voice."

"Bill, IF you lower your voice, THEN I'll listen to what you have to say. BUT IF you keep on yelling, THEN I have other things to do."

Roadblocks. Okay, so far so good. You got the words out. Now what? Will the person automatically lie down and play dead? Fat chance. He'll come out fighting with sticks and stones and names you won't believe. Fury will rise sky-high until you either buckle under or use your stamina to withstand the attack. If you've come this far, you can go further. It gets easier as you take more control—healthy control. You can do it!

The way around unfriendly replies to your DESC is by handling *roadblocks*. Roadblocks are nasty remarks intended to dislodge your assertive efforts. The offensive person can't believe you said what you said. He is absolutely stunned. Shocked, he reacts defensively, because he doesn't know what else to do. Another part of his reaction is to push you back to being meek and mild, so he can be on top again. He may say and do these things to you:

- accuse you of lying
- turn your statements around and say you're at fault
- scream louder
- threaten you
- hit or almost hit you
- break objects in the house
- laugh at you
- embarrass you publicly

All of these reactions are because the person does not know what to do. You've just become another person; in his eyes you're the man on the moon. And how would you react to an extra-terrestrial at first meeting? You wouldn't. You'd be dumbfounded. That's how the offensive person feels. You've caught him off guard, and so he says and does what is intuitive. But don't fall for it. Don't get swept up in the roadblocks just because they sound threatening or frightening. Realize your best approach is just to say, "That's not the point, the point is ..." and return to the DESC format.

After repeating the DESC format twice, maybe three times, and even the consequences are failing, all is not lost. Just bail out politely by saying: "I'm sorry you feel that way."

This phrase is not avoidance or escape behavior. You've already expressed yourself, made your point clear, offered a compromise, stated consequences, and endured roadblock after roadblock. Don't kill yourself trying to "win the game." There is no game. All you wanted to do was hear yourself and have the person hear you speak your piece. And you've done that very well. Don't push it further for now. If that's all that transpires, so be it. Let it rest. There'll be plenty of other occasions to practice this skill. And on every occasion you'll get better.

STEP 5
No More Fear of Rejection

> *If I could do more,*
> *If I could work harder,*
> *If I could love stronger,*
> *Then I'd never feel hurt,*
> *And never feel alone.*

Yes, you would. You always would. And it's not your fault. You're not the mighty oak, towering above all other trees in the forest. Higher than mountains, bigger and better than all of nature's best. You're not impervious to pain and suffering. You feel it all the time. And it's not because you're weaker, smaller, or sadder than most people. It's because you *care*.

You care so much about everybody and everything that there are too many people to share your caring with. So, you try to be selective. You show caring to your spouse, your children, your friends, your parents, your siblings. They all get a piece of the pie. They enjoy it. You don't. Nothing is left for you. And when they want more pieces of the pie, there's no more to go around. You're empty. Even if you fake it and give love even when you've been tapped dry of love, they still want more. You can't keep up with their appetites. They're addicted to your love. They're addicted to your caring. And you're the supplier. You keep their addiction going.

Only when you say, "enough," either for the moment or forever, do things go crazy. You take your love and caring away, and they feel deprived. They feel sad. They get mad. This trips off a reaction called *rejection*.

Rejection is tuning you out and turning you off because something happened. And you feel that what happened was your fault. Instantly you blame yourself for being too pushy, too insensitive, too full of pain, and for causing grief in another person. "For that person to reject me, I really must have overdone it this time—God help me." Rejection turns into abandonment. "Now I've lost that person forever!" And it feels that permanent.

Rejection is always perceived as negative. Like it's the plague. But it's not the plague. Rejection is oxygen. You must breathe it to stay alive. It is a *must*. You must learn to feel it, tolerate it, and accept rejection as a normal reaction to life's surprises. Rejection becomes a positive dose of esteem-building medicine once you conquer your fears and can face rejection like a cold icy day. It's only bad if you hate cold and ice. But if you learn to like ice, learn how to use ice, suddenly the knot in your stomach disappears. You skate, you ski, you make cold and ice your friend. The same is true of rejection. Learn that rejection is a normal part of daily living, and it will become your most intimate companion as you feel healthy and try new things.

So, welcome to Step 4, *No more fear of rejection*.

Facing the Need for Hurt

It is easy to upset people. Any little thing can set off a chain reaction of accusations, anger, and being ignored by the people you've tried most to make happy. Now they're not happy. And that's good. They need to be unhappy for you to break free of guilt.

Why you must annoy people. You must annoy people so that you can:

- break the cycle of their expecting you to do whatever they ask.
- force people to be responsible for themselves.
- force people to take you seriously.
- look to others for your dependent needs.

Why you must be hated. What if the annoyance turns sour? Suppose your family and friends are so bitterly angry that they hate you. What then? So let them hate you. They will not hate you forever. Hate is never forever. Hate is temporary. It acts like a roadblock that seduces you into feeling ashamed and going back to your old habits. But you won't go back. Never again. Those habits are history.

Look at hate, not as bad, but as a landmark of something good. Hate means you've started the ball rolling and you're into the first phase of freeing yourself of guilt. You must get people annoyed, angry and hateful so that they will:

- take out their frustrations on other people
- learn you won't budge unless they behave differently
- start viewing you as *a person entitled to respect*

Why you can't be fooled by what they do to others. "They'll take out their frustrations on other people? No way!" That's your immediate reaction. "Why should other people be dumped on? It was my fault, not theirs." Your fear is that other people get the brunt of anger you caused in the aggressive person. You feel for those other people. You want to rescue them before it's too late. You also worry those people will be angry with you. Somehow, someway, they'll find out who put a thorn under the aggressor's feet. That's all it will take for them to hate you forever.

Trying to forecast who is affected, who might be angry, and what might happen is a bad habit. It traps you into the same mistake of "reading into things" without knowing the facts. Even if you did know the facts—"Yes, they really are annoyed at me for getting that guy angry"—*who cares?* What is so horrible about causing a chain reaction of anger from one person to another? The answer: There's nothing wrong with it.

It's part of feeling alive, of realizing your strength depends on detaching from fearful thoughts; this biggest fearful thought is that you caused everybody's misery. Hurt and anger that other people feel because you stood up for yourself go with the territory and you must let the angry people deal with the anger on their own. It's not your fault, it's not your anger, and it's not your job to clean up the mess.

Why you can't base self-love on being loved. Don't play "mirror, mirror on the wall...." Your answer will always be: "I'm the fairest of them all according to how much I'm loved." You may care too much what your intimate or friends think of you. In your eyes they like you or dislike you based on what you do for them, how you do it, and how you avoid conflict. When you get rejected, however, this all changes.

Now you've rubbed them the wrong way. They'd rather be with somebody else. They've put you in layaway until you apologize or come back on your hands and knees begging for forgiveness. You don't want to stoop this low, but inside you feel emotionally scared, abandoned, and fearful nobody ever will take their place. You perceive yourself as good only as long as they do. Once they drop you, you drop yourself. It's that quick.

But who you are and why you are special cannot be person-based. Your life revolves around routines that are entirely your own. Your choices of clothes, television shows, foods, etc., must be based on personal preferences. Watch out for being influenced too much. If somebody says to you, "You're only my friend if you watch *Roseanne* and *Home Improvement.*" You can probably handle it. Whether you like or dislike these shows, you probably won't hurry home to watch these shows so that you can keep this person as a friend. You'd react the same way if this friend insisted that people who eat Slim Fast bars are fake dieters and are not her friends. Does that mean you'll throw out your year's stock of Slim Fast bars? I doubt it.

On television show and food choices you can hold your own. That's simple. You're the king of the castle, and you can resist petty obligations, realizing how irrelevant they are to your personality. So, what's the difference if the person says, "Fine, only this time you come over to my house for the party," or, "That outfit doesn't look good on you," or, "Take more bowling lessons or else you're not playing on the team." These threats sound more overpowering and compel you to instantly comply or else face friendship abandonment. Yes, you agree to the party at her house; yes, you agree your outfit doesn't look good; and yes, you agree that your bowling stinks.

Their advice *feels right* because these statements do not apply to routines. Non-routines are up for grabs. Your image of yourself comes from the image people make of your non-routines, of your daily activities, and suddenly you feel they know more about you than you do. You trust them more than you trust yourself. That's because you don't want to risk being a maverick, a show-off, and possibly make the wrong choice.

But here's the flaw. Their ideas are just as wrong. Nobody gave them a perfect score on advice. In fact, advice people give you, no matter how confident it sounds, is only that: advice. Their advice may not fit your needs, and may possibly be bad for you. If a person said he can drink three beers in an hour, does that mean you can, or should, do the same? Of course not. Your body handles the beer differently. And so the same is true for all ideas people give you. Never believe anybody until you have all the facts. And if doing what they want means they'll love you more, then you don't need *their* love.

You need *your* love. Self-love comes from saying *no*. Self-love comes from trying out bits and pieces of your own ideas, some borrowed from others and some constructed entirely on your own, full of imperfections and lots of risks.

Risking Disapproval

You can practice making people reject you. Remember, you want people to reject you so you can learn not to depend on their love, friendship, or other promises to feel important. Independence fosters self-love and ambition.

Try to:

Change life routines. This means you should modify a daily habit. Things you routinely do around which other people revolve and feel comfortable should be changed in minor ways. For example, instead of bathing in the evening, do so in the morning. Instead of retiring late at night, go to bed earlier. Intimates affected by your shift in routines must immediately change their routines to some extent, causing inconvenience.

And that's exactly what you want to cause them—inconvenience.

Change your opinions. If you're a Democrat, try taking a Republican stand. Interject more opinions on a daily basis. Disagree about topics you typically agree on or ignore as unimportant. Your increased communication may startle intimates and friends, possibly annoy them, and consequently make them feel uneasy about what will come out of your mouth next. That's good: keep them guessing. You've been predictable for too long. Now it's time for a change. Make them wonder what's going on and realize they have to change their own behavior in response to the new you.

Change your personality. You already have a wonderful personality. You are probably afraid to try being different, in case it backfires and inconveniences or hurts people you care about. Now is your chance to risk minor deviations in behavior in spite of what other people think. How you talk, what you say, how you dress, your laughter, your working behavior—all are good candidates for variation. Experiment with new characteristics you admire in other people or think would be fun, but have been too reserved to try. Experimenting with new behavior is actually normal during mid-childhood and teenage years. But your early and late adolescence may have been busy times for other things that robbed you of this chance. Or, your parents may not have let you experiment with behavior because it inconvenienced them too much.

But now you can. Nobody said the person you know as yourself today has to remain packaged the same way for life. You can change anything, along any dimension, and according to any creative image, as long as you're making these changes because *you* want to.

Change your relationship. If you instantly want contact with rejection, try breaking up with your current bad-news relationship. You don't want the relationship anymore and are tired of pretending tomorrow will be different. So, end it. Step 10 tells you more about how to do this.

Letting It Go—Detachment

You've pushed the button that says, "Go." Now there's no turning back. It's straight down the middle from here. And you can get there by letting your guilt go and becoming detached.

Becoming detached. Detaching means you'll no longer take on other people's feelings—you'll only deal with your own. You may have thought *detached* meant feeling nothing; being numb. Wrong. There's a danger in numbing your feelings. Fear and panic paralyze your feelings now just as they did when you were growing up or in broken relationships. You mistakenly learned to turn off, and tune out all conflict, criticism, and rejection before it dug too deep. That feeling is one of helplessness; you insulate yourself from more hate and danger by hiding behind a huge wall.

The right way to be detached is not to build a wall. You're not insulating yourself from hatred. Instead, you're allowing your personal wants, feelings, and ideas to be more important than the wants, feelings, and ideas of another person. You project yourself onto an imaginary screen, and you're larger than life and more impressive than anybody around you. For that moment you have permission to be arrogant. Like the stars of the Golden Age of Hollywood, you are the envy of all those around you. You have an "other-worldly" characteristic, and nothing can shake this wonderful feeling you have about yourself.

Once you achieve this image of yourself, you begin to inventory why you're better than the other person. You come up with reasons such as these.

I'm BETTER than this person because I wouldn't say what he's saying.

I'm BETTER than this person because I wouldn't act the way he's acting.

I'm BETTER than this person because I can remain calm and in control.

Why Rejection Doesn't Equal Abandonment

You feel on top of the world. You're *Number 1*. There's no kidding around this time. You're serious about staying at the top. But what can you do about those persistent fears. Fears that scream at you, saying, "Who are you fooling? You just pushed everyone out of your life, and nobody will want you anymore!" You try ignoring this irritating feeling but it doesn't go away. Night after night it returns, like a ghost, determined to destroy your peace of mind.

You're thinking that *abandonment* is the price you pay for being a hot shot and making people reject you; that rejection equals abandonment. But it's not true. You're not abandoned by anybody. You've just forced people to stop and realize what abusive things they've done to you for many years and that you're not going to take it anymore.

You're not alone. You're never alone. Loneliness is for people who breathe if somebody tells them to breathe. You, on the other hand, breathe or do anything because you've finally unleashed the remarkable person deep inside you who wants to experiment with life and behavior. You can make your own fun by going to places you previously thought were off limits. You can meet new people you never dared to talk to, thinking they were better than you, or fearing your friends would disown you if they learned of it.

Try this short exercise. Fill in the blanks as you ask yourself, "What is it I really want to do that everybody thinks I shouldn't?"

1. _____
2. _____
3. _____

Now ask yourself, "Who are the people I really want to meet or talk with even though my (spouse, friends, family) forbid it?"

1. _____
2. _____
3. _____

Now, re-read your answers. You really want to try these things. They're not just words on a page. Figure out when you can go to the places or do the things you wrote down in your first list. For the second list, be realistic. You may not meet a movie star tomorrow. But there are plenty of other people, perhaps people in certain professions, you can meet very soon. Think about ways of making those contacts come true.

Fighting off self-blame. You're not going to blame yourself for feeling abandoned. Remember, you *want* certain people gone because they have exploited or abused you. Keeping abusers and exploiters around is like asking a criminal to take everything in your house as long as he keeps you company. Don't inflict torture on yourself for the sake of relieving guilt. Fight off self-blame by blaming the other person. Identify what that person said or did to you and, in your mind, submit it on a list to your mental jury. Find the person guilty as charged and sentence this person to banishment.

Finding fault also means telling other people why you are angry at the person who supposedly abandoned you. Always speak positively to yourself about the situation—why it's better this way, and how you're a better person for it. You're not abandoned, you're liberated.

Starting over. Treat rejection not as abandonment, but as a door to opportunity. It's like being fired from a job. Either you wallow in grief over your lost income and terrible work habits or you gear up for a fresh start. Be optimistic. Plan new approaches to old problems. Nobody says that starting over must mean doing the same things over again. It doesn't. It means creating a different horizon of hope with completely revised strategies and rejuvenation of energy. You don't need the same old person to make you start over again. Motivation comes from what you can do, not from somebody else who can help do it for you.

It's okay to be wrong. Okay, so you reacted irrationally at times. Your behavior damaged the relationship as much as the destructive things the other person did. Should you automatically apologize to the person in hopes of reconciliation? No, not always; not if you benefited from the rejection; not if it opened your eyes to terrible abuses and ugly co-dependency habits, and made you take a new look at yourself. These are the advantages of rejection. If you feel any one of these benefits the rejection must stay in place.

There are times when rejection is completely normal, and it's okay to be wrong. Marriages are a good example. Normal couples have arguments. Mistakes you and your spouse make in the argument may cause resentment. Perhaps you used four-letter words; maybe your spouse shouted the whole time. Nobody is perfect. There are no ground rules for perfect arguments. Arguing always goes awry because tensions run a course of heated emotions and shifts in control: now you've got it, now you don't. The pendulum swings unpredictably and continuously.

You can apologize for your behavior as long as your spouse apologies as well. It must be reciprocal. But that's all you're apologizing for. It's okay to cause your spouse grief; it's okay to disagree with what your spouse says; it's okay that the argument occurred. You're not sorry for arguing; you're just sorry for being rude.

Basic Relaxation When Feeling Rejected

Stress from rejection is hardest to relieve in your body. Tension you feel as a result of conflict and criticism quickly takes hold and rises uncontrollably. Your insides turn to fire, burning like an inferno from your head to toe. You feel flush all over, possibly coupled with dizziness or weakness. All you want to do is sit down or escape the situation. But you can't; that's what makes body stress worse. You try fighting the stress off by yelling, crying, and tuning yourself out. You repeat your efforts again and again. Nothing works. It seems hopeless.

Most of you can relax on your own in a number of ways. Many ways are routine—watching television, taking a nap, reading a book, cooking, eating, and having sex. All of these are natural tension-lowering activities. Tension relief becomes routine, because your body simply cannot endure constant muscle pressure; it can only take so much pressure before it collapses. You feel exhausted, mentally beat, and emotionally drained. Taking a breather is a matter of physical and mental survival.

Some of you are not so good at relaxing on your own. You have to be dead tired before you finally surrender to your insides and say, "Okay, you win." Otherwise you run like a chicken with its head cut off, doing anything and everything you can to avoid feeling rejected. You distract yourself with a million activities. But there's another way to overcome rejection. It's more direct and physically more healing to your body. You can induce relaxation. There's nothing hypnotic about it. You simply take a moment out of your day, whether at home, work or on the run, and use one of the two methods described below:

Visual imagery. Visual imagery means precisely that. You imagine in your "mind's eye" a quiet, calm place where you think you can relax. On a beach, in bed, on a vacation—any fantasy that lasts a few seconds will distract you from anxious thoughts and interrupt muscle pressure. Try this while you're waiting in a grocery line, while waiting in a doctor's office, and especially any time you think about the person who rejected you.

Use visual imagery correctly. NEVER conjure up memories of being with the person who rejected you. NEVER imagine yourself more productive, nicer to people, and making more friends. NEVER imagine yourself relaxed only because you're doing things for somebody else. NEVER imagine yourself relaxed because somebody is catering to you.

Muscle relaxation. Muscle relaxation is more specific and probably your best bet for on-the-spot tension relief. First, identify where your body feels tense: face, neck, shoulder blades, etc. Do a quick inventory to pinpoint where the stresses originate.

Second, momentarily increase the pressure in those muscle areas. There are many ways to do this. Make your muscles feel tighter. Then release the pressure quickly. That fast release gives you a strong contrast between tense muscles and loose muscles. The chart on the next page gives you some ideas about ways to tighten and release key muscle areas.

AREA	TIGHTEN	RELEASE
Forehead	Wrinkle brow; raise eyebrows	Now, let go (repeat)
Eyes	Close eyes tight	Now, let go (repeat)
Mouth (teeth)	Push tongue up against roof of mouth or clench teeth	Now, let go (repeat)
Cheek bone	Smile and try to touch corners of mouth to ears	Now, let go (repeat)
Neck	Bend to chest	Now, let go (repeat)
Stomach	Make a knot in your stomach	Now, let go (repeat)
Shoulders	Bring shoulders up to touch ears	Now, let go (repeat)
Arms	Make a muscle	Now, let go (repeat)
Wrists	Bend palms toward you	Now, let go (repeat)
Hands	Make a fist like squeezing a tennis ball	Now, let go (repeat)
Fingers	Stretch fingers like they're being pulled	Now, let go (repeat)
Thighs	Lift legs 3 inches off ground and hold for 5 seconds	Now, let go (repeat)
Legs	Press legs flat on the floor	Now, let go (repeat)
Feet	Point heel away and push	Now, let go (repeat)
Toes	Stretch toes like they're being pulled	Now, let go (repeat)

Removing tension may produce a warm, tingling sensation. It's almost the way you feel when your foot falls asleep. Don't shake away the tingling sensation. It's supposed to be there. You can bring on the tingling and calming sensation anywhere: inside the house, outside, or at work. One place is as good as the next. Some of the tighten-release exercises can be varied for privacy. For example, for shoulders, you may not be able to bring your shoulder blades up to your ears. That's a bit conspicuous. It's not that you care what other people think, but it may interfere with the situation you're trying to control better. Instead, stretch your shoulders back, pulling your elbows slightly behind your back. Similar variations are possible for legs, thighs, and neck.

This quick relaxation method can free you from leftover anxiety after rejection. You can combat feeling alone, abandoned, and guilty by eliminating stress in your body. Unrelieved stress piles up and can magnify your misperception of internal pain as something you deserved, because you got yourself into this mess. But nothing could be so far from the truth. The truth is that you are proud of rejection because it graduates you to new levels of independence. And you're prepared to make that independence last, no matter what happens.

STEP 6
No More Fear of Failure (The Impostor Syndrome)

You spend many sleepless nights pondering all the possible ways you can "make things better" by fixing things you do wrong—how you talk, walk, dress, and even eat. You find something wrong with everything. Nothing goes right. How could it? You always do things wrong and everybody knows it.

Or so you think. Feeling guilty because you think you fail at everything is painful. No sooner do you see a light at the end of the tunnel than that tunnel caves in. You're always doomed from the start. There's no Midas touch for you. Everything you touch turns bad. And why do you have such bad luck? Is it inherited? Are you the product of bad genes? No, probably not. Maybe it's something else. But what?

The answer lies in one simple word: FEAR.

You fear making a mistake. In fact, you're terrified of making a mistake, because it might bring the posse down on your trail. You'll be hounded by criticism and rejection. And there's bound to be conflict—all because you made mistakes that were preventable. You're paranoid about errors. You're hypersensitive about looking stupid, incompetent, and imperfect. So, you have a choice. Either you keep on the look-out for all possible errors you'll ever make, or you forget the fears and just relax, risking the awful consequences you believe are in store for ignoring the bad things you do.

You need to relieve yourself from 24-hour guard duty against making mistakes. That's what Step 6 is all about. It forces you to accept your mistakes. It lets your faults be exposed for all to see, and finally lets you trash that self-image of inferiority when mistakes overwhelm you. So, first, let's get an idea of what type of mistakes we're talking about. That means learning about *the impostor syndrome*. Then, you'll find easy ways to stop fearing your mistakes and trying to be perfect.

Mistakes are:
- Not living up to what you said you would do
- Finding an error in what you say or do
- Doing things that make you feel inferior compared to other people
- Doing or saying things that humiliate, upset, or embarrass you
- Repeating behaviors you feel should be corrected by now
- Saying or doing things people say are bad and need correction

You hide mistakes by:
- Apologizing
- Defending yourself
- Pretending you know something when you don't
- Replaying the mistake in your head, on your mental movie screen. You add new words, change your actions, and try redoing the situation until mistakes disappear.
- Becoming self-critical. You criticize yourself for being so stupid and careless. You attack your credibility, call yourself names, and scold yourself for not preventing the mistake.
- Blaming other people. It's their fault for not preventing your mistake. You accuse significant others more than you accuse friends. People close to you should have alerted you ahead of time that things were going wrong.

Does it matter how many things you do wrong? No. Does it matter how big or small the mistakes are? No. Does it matter who spots the mistakes? Yes.

You've Been Caught!

You feel shame when you are caught doing something you believe is wrong. Somebody—mother, father, sibling, spouse, or child—saw you doing something wrong, and you feel like it's the end of the world. "What will they think of me?" Your perceptions of yourself become important. You want to maintain a strong, positive self-image so people will like you, want you, and ask you to do things for them. Jeopardizing that trust means you are *no good*.

The fear of being caught takes three forms. (1) You monitor yourself. (2) You scan other people's behavior. And, (3) you feel like an impostor.

First, you know you hate feeling ashamed. So, anything you can do to monitor yourself may prevent shame. You watch what you say, how you act or react, and become obsessively careful not to upset people around you. Self-monitoring lasts all day.

Second, you are constantly scanning the thoughts and actions of other people so you can strategically figure out when they are wise to your mistakes. You break down a person's life into segments of prediction. You become your own fortune teller, anticipating what the person will say or do, and how you'll intercept these actions. You know their habits inside and out. You've connected into their circuit and are ready for a glitch in the system. You know exactly what triggers the person; what mistakes he hates or tolerates. You map out his every move, from beginning to end. If anything happens, you're absolutely ready for it.

Third, you're always looking behind your back. You know it's just a matter of time before someone, somewhere will uncover the truth about you. You feel the "other shoe will fall any minute." A person will point out that everything you thought you were is a lie. It will all come out in the open. You're a fake, a phony—an impostor. You've created an artificial shell of confidence that will finally be torn away, and the real you will be exposed.

Feeling like an impostor means you constantly fear people will discover you don't really know what you're doing and that you'll be the laughing stock of the universe. Ambitions you embark on cannot escape this fear. Take Sheila, for example. She started a resume business. She tailor-made people's resumes, undercutting and outdoing the competition. Her products were phenomenal. Her customers loved her work. But Sheila thought they were just being polite. Sheila believed her work was inferior; she felt she was an imposter, and that competitors would one day reveal that fact.

No matter how successful Sheila became, she never attributed her success to the quality of her work. She was too ashamed for that. It felt more normal to think other people in the business belonged there, but she didn't.

Fear of being exposed comes from being criticized and teased as a child. You heard bad things said about you and your efforts—no matter what you did or how often you did it. It happened so regularly that it seemed commonplace—it seemed true. You believed every word of it. And why shouldn't you? Your parents said it to you. And you believed your parents. Today, as an adult, nobody criticizes you much at all. Your parents probably don't constantly put you down, either. But it doesn't matter. You do it yourself. You provide yourself with the criticism. You say harsh, unforgiving, demeaning things to yourself. This sends you into a tail spin. You get angry and defensive. You cry, or feel depressed, acting exactly like you did when scolded as a child. Although you're older, the habit of hating mistakes and making yourself emotionally pay for mistakes endures.

So, get rid of that fear of mistakes. *First,* tell yourself perfectionism doesn't work; no one is perfect. *Second,* risk new situations where you expose your actions and words. *Third,* accept and solicit compliments, drawing attention to yourself. *Fourth,* reverse the impostor feeling.

Why Perfectionism Doesn't Work

Striving to be perfect is no good. You never work so hard for the positive rewards. You do it because you want to avoid feeling ashamed, criticized, and rejected. Spending 3 hours to make your hair and make-up look "just right" is *avoidance*. It's not vanity. You simply don't want somebody saying it looks bad. Spending 3 hours an evening playing tennis to improve your swing is *avoidance*. It's not for love of tennis. It's from a fear of looking stupid on the tennis court. Reactions to fear mobilize you in all sorts of directions—obsessions, compulsions, and needlessly re-doing things to get them right.

You create a standard of what's right based on that parental voice in your mind or what others tell you. Your sense of right is what others say is right. This leads you to work harder and harder at achieving this standard—no matter the emotional cost. But here's the irony. Extremes of effort always backfire. The results of your effort never meet your standard.

The more you try to perfect something, the more you make mistakes. It never fails. The more time and energy you spend trying to perfect something, the more you make *new* mistakes. You dot all your *i*'s and cross all your *t*'s, and you think you've finally got it. But you've only made it worse. For example, why do you spend hours fiddling around with a car engine you know nothing about? Why do you persist? Because you can't admit defeat—failure is hard to swallow. So you struggle angrily, yelling and screaming until you get it right. But the more you poke around, the worse the problem gets. You break a tool, smash a finger, and the engine still doesn't run.

Extra effort equals higher demand. Lots of time and energy delude you into thinking it made a difference. But it didn't. By mistake you spent so much time fixing that engine that now you think you always have to spend lots of time doing things or they're not done right. And spending hours on projects for other people is just as bad. It's not a one-time thing. If it takes you 10 hours to clean their house, they'll expect you to spend 10 hours on it the next time, or even 11 or 12 hours.

You figure it this way: "Hey, if I spent 3 hours and it came out good, twice the time will make it better." Wrong, twice the time and you're bound to be angrier, more tired, and more down on yourself.

Extreme effort signals avoidance of other issues. You work diligently to avoid doing other things you don't want to do. Homework is a good example. College is fun, but only on Friday night. Writing papers and studying for tests are awful. So, you might kill 5 or 10 hours cleaning your apartment, scrubbing every nook and cranny, just to delay doing your homework. The irony is that once you begin your homework, you put in another 5 to 10 hours getting it perfect.

Instead

Let mistakes happen. Start your day off by saying, "Whatever happens will happen—or NBD (No Big Deal). It's no big deal if things go wrong." From baking a cake that flops to never fixing that engine, who cares? Not you. Just let it happen.

- *Don't* get upset.
- *Don't* correct it (not just yet).
- *Don't* blame others for it.
- *Don't* hide it.

Just walk away from the mistake. Laugh about it, then:
- Tell somebody about the mistake you made.
- Put a limit on the time you spend to fix it (15 minute maximum).
- Ask someone to help you fix the mistake.

When you see a mistake coming ... don't stop it! Some mistakes just happen. You can't prevent them, and you never see them coming. That's when you say NBD. But sometimes you can see a mistake coming and instead of interceding to stop it, just let it happen. Tell yourself that it's going to be okay. When you see the mistake coming ...

- Stop what you're doing and let it happen.
- Laugh about it.
- Tell somebody around you about the mistake.
- Put a limit on the time you spend correcting the mistake.

You can't allow all mistakes to occur, of course. If your car is sliding on ice headed for another car, you want to prevent the mistake. You're not interested in turning a collision into a learning experience. However, few errors in your life are actually this monumental. They may feel monumental, but they are really minor.

Lower the standard. You're only as good as you think you are. But what if your standard for *being good* is very high? Then you'll never think you're good. You'll always be below standard. The way you raise your kids—below standard. The way you perform your job—below standard. The way you make love—way below standard. Nothing reaches close to standard because *your standard doesn't exist.* It never did and it never will. You only think it does. Standards, like criticism, come from feeling inadequate in childhood. You were told to do something better. So, you tried. But it wasn't good enough. You tried again. It still didn't pass the test. Again, you tried. Your mother said, "Fine, that'll do." But you knew it wasn't fine. Nothing was fine.

Nothing was ever fine; there was never a right way to do it; there was only the way your parents wanted it done. And that standard fell somewhere between "Do it like I do it" and "I don't know, but I know what you're doing is wrong." A standard only existed in the mind of your parents. It rarely, if ever, was demonstrated for you to copy. It was an abstract, very obscure standard. Nobody was ever able to grasp it. That is why you never reached that standard in childhood—how could you reach it? It was a figment of your parent's imagination.

And today it is a figment of your imagination. That is, until you dismantle it. Remove the obscure, imprecise standard by creating a new standard. Here's how to do it:

1. Do something you usually do. For example, bake a potato.

2. Don't change the way you normally do it. Just do it.

3. If you don't know when to end the task, set an end point. Set it by time or amount done. For example, for the potato, put it in the microwave for a certain number of minutes.

4. Inspect the task at the end of the selected time period. Feel the potato. Have you accomplished what you need or want in that situation? For instance, taste the potato. Does it taste done? If it does, the amount of time and effort put into preparing that potato is the new standard for baking a potato. You don't need it any better. If it tastes raw or undercooked, put the potato back in the microwave and add half-minutes to the baking time. Now repeat the taste-test.

When what you've done satisfies your basic needs for the moment, then you've created a new standard. Don't mentally correct the process or start criticizing yourself because the potato is a bit squishy, just accept the potato the way it is.

Let others make mistakes. Victory over mistakes is accepting your failures. You can stand tall and say, "Hey, NBD—it's no big deal if I put too much shampoo on my hair or overwatered the plants. Things happen." You feel confident, able to speak about your errors in regular dialogue: no apologies, no defensive remarks, no accusations. You think you've licked the impostor-syndrome.

But then it happens. You notice how impatient you get when other people make mistakes. In fact, you can't stand their being so stupid. The mistakes they make are so preventable that anybody in his right mind should know better. Not really. At one time you didn't know better. Now you do. Now you know better than to terrorize yourself. So, you must extend the same courtesy to other people.

It is easy to project your own faults onto another person. This most often happens when you stop dumping on yourself. You relieve yourself by finding another scapegoat. You almost *look* for mistakes other people make to lift yourself above everyone else. That assures you that you're better. But you're only buying time. The moment people are not around—when scapegoats are gone—fault-finding will revert to you. You'll become your own scapegoat once again.

But not if you act now. Take these steps when you spot a fault in somebody else.

1. Ignore it.

2. If you can't ignore it, point it out in objective terms. Describe only what you saw or heard, not why you think it happened. Suppose your friend dropped her napkin on the floor. Say, "Hey, Joan, your napkin fell on the floor." DO NOT SAY: "Hey, clumsy, can't you even hold onto a napkin?"

3. Do not offer to fix the mistake. Let the other person deal with it without your help.

4. If the person laughs about it or shrugs it off, you do the same thing.

No matter how upset you get inside; no matter how wrong or socially inane the act was; no matter how stupid you think the person is, just let it go. Nobody asked for your opinion about the mistake. So, don't give one. If you do, you're only making someone else feel bad so you can feel good because it wasn't you who made the error.

Be proud of the mistake. There are many things in life to be proud of. But usually you can't think of even one. Pride seems reserved for the "great strides in life that only great people make." (Abraham Lincoln's *Gettysburg Address*—now that was something to be proud of!) You put *pride* on the shelf along with other never-to-earn trophies such as being perfect, being smart, and being happy. The trouble is that pride becomes obscure like the rest of your standards.

You can change this by redefining what you call *pride*. A proud moment is any personal learning experience you have without feeling guilty. Pride is accepting the trials and errors of daily risks, and feeling you made progress trying something very new and very scary. Pride is:

1. Making a mistake and calling it a mistake without calling yourself a bad name.

2. Accepting the outcome of anything you try a step toward learning something new.

3. Laughing about disappointments no matter how large or small.

4. Liking a person in spite of the mistakes the person makes.

5. Taking new risks, knowing ahead of time that you're guaranteed to stumble at least a few times.

Exposing Vulnerability in Risk Situations

It's time to show your true colors. Unravel the real you hiding underneath that impostor's mask. Step away from the shield that protects you from shame. You can do it. You can already accept mistakes. So, now comes the part where you tell others how well you can accept mistakes.

Telling things that embarrass you. Admit personal embarrassment. Initiate a conversation about something you said or did that make you feel stupid. "You won't believe what I did. I watered a fake plant!" After sharing the story, let others react to it naturally, without buffering their remarks.

DO NOT:

1. Criticize yourself after admitting you did something wrong.

2. Justify why you did it.

3. Perceive their laughter or teasing as rejection.

4. Find fault in those who laugh at or tease you.

Telling things that are negative. Self put-downs are easy for you. They may have become your favorite past-time. Now you get to put yourself down in a constructive and healthy way—a way used by most people at one time or another. First, initiate a conversation about something you did wrong. What you did does not have to be humiliating; it is just a mistake. Describe it briefly, without long-winded details to help the listener understand why you did it. *Why* you did it is irrelevant. What is important is that you risk telling about it.

After you tell what you did wrong, make one of these responses.

- Say, "Well, *things* happen to everybody."
- Listen to the reactions of others.
- Resist justifying or clarifying the details so they can truly digest the full situation. However they comprehend it is perfectly fine.
- Let the topic be dropped.

You are tempted to call people back after they walk away. You feel an addictive need to make sure they still like you or think you're competent. Reaching out for security by asking, "You don't really think I'm crazy, do you?" invites people to make more of what you said than they would have before you asked. Resist your compulsion. Don't force them to say you're okay after you spill your guts. Unloading personal information necessitates this risk; you must undergo emotional detoxification of anxiety, worry, and grief without getting relief from these symptoms if tomorrow's efforts are to be easier.

Volunteering for things you don't know how to do. Step into failure-producing situations by agreeing to do things you lack total competency in. If you know nothing about automobile engines, agree to help your friend tune-up his car or change the anti-freeze. Do you lack experience making dinner reservations? Take it upon yourself to call for reservations. You'll stumble over your words. You'll look and sound confused, and probably be scared. You may goof it up completely. But force yourself to repeat your efforts until you get it right. For every success, a thousand errors may occur.

But that's normal. Let it happen. You'll feel humiliated and angry because you're being pushed out of your comfort zone; the protective seal around you is tearing. You're deep in the trenches of vulnerability. Stay in those trenches long enough to try the new challenge—no matter what the outcome is. End products are less important than fighting off the urge to escape the process. Win that fight by sticking it out. Continue exploring different ways to accomplish the challenging task, testing out old and new skills. You won't lose; you'll just finish the race farther back. And that's better than dropping out of the race early because you get cold feet.

Be follower or leader, whichever is more anxiety producing. Your tendency is to do both. Some people afraid of failure take on the *control stick.* Control prevents others from seeing the real you. Still others prefer a low profile, preventing fault-exposure by doing as little as possible, or by following the leader. Whichever is your gateway to comfort, choose the opposite one.

If you are usually a leader, try being a follower for a group project. That means no input from you. You remain uninvolved until or unless asked to do certain things by the leader. Forget how *wrong* or *stupid* the leader's directions are. Forget that you could probably do the job better than the leader. Forget that, doing it the leader's way, things may go wrong or remedial efforts may be needed to repair damage caused by stupid mistakes.

If you are typically a follower, raise your hand to volunteer in a leadership capacity. That means taking on the responsibility of a large job involving other people who you must (a) assign to tasks, (b) get angry at, (c) organize on a schedule, and (d) act as troubleshooter for. Ask for help from other people at first, but not all the time. Try it by yourself. Make a mini-disaster of the situation if you have to. Just do it yourself.

If you usually neither follow nor lead groups, but rarely get involved in any capacity, now is the time to seek membership in organizations. Groups of all sorts—recreational, educational, religious—offer opportunities to exchange ideas with people. Join at least one group where you must contribute input to a decision.

When you find your niche, blend into the group by helping out at social or organized functions. **Never**, however, try to guarantee approval from these new groups by:

- telling them your life story
- enlisting their support in your grief so they will understand why you do "goofy" things

- becoming the group mascot and taking orders from every person there, so they'll like you

Seek counseling. Risk-taking includes the choice to call a therapist. This is a big step toward a fantastic goal, but it usually means a personal sacrifice. You sacrifice your privacy—your inner secrets kept locked away so nobody would know your weak points. Now you might release them; but it's not like opening Pandora's Box. Nothing bad happens. Secrets you let out are like germs passing from your infected body. You become healthy by removing germs and learning how to keep those germs away. You become immunized. And therapy is your personal vaccine. You prevent secrets from cluttering up your mind and causing you emotional unrest.

Accepting and Soliciting Compliments

The next toughest hang-up to overcome is hating your looks. You hate to look at yourself in the mirror; you hate to listen to yourself on the tape-recorder; and you hate people taking your picture. "Can't people just leave me alone?"

No, they can't. They don't want to because you're too handsome or too beautiful for them ignore. "Oh that's a bunch of ____."

You turn off compliments like you turn off a light switch. All the electrical power in you goes off instantly, without any traces of energy. All black, with no feeling. Inside you feel empty. That's because you never heard compliments growing up or there was a steep price to pay for being complimented. It taught you to distrust every nice thing anybody ever said about you. But now you can change this around.

Size up the situation. Figure out when you can interject a phrase or two about yourself. Don't worry for the moment about what you'll say; just focus on when you can say it. Size up the situation by listening to another person talk. Natural breaths in between chatter are perfect times to chime in. So are occasions when the speaker is changing the topic.

Convert the dialogue. To convert a dialogue, listen to what a person is saying and then add something about yourself to the conversation. It can be opposite to what the speaker says or a new feature. But your input must be something positive about you. For example:

Speaker: "Hey, do you see how wet it is out there? I hate that."

You: "I think it kind of looks nice out there. The wet doesn't bother me."

In effect, you're drawing brief attention to yourself by describing some positive feature you have. Your reply is brief and never defensive. It's just a simple self-promo statement.

Shift the dialogue. This is where you shift the focus from the speaker to yourself by keeping the conversation alive. Make the speaker become a listener. Interrupt the speaker when the speaker takes a natural breath. That's your cue to move in. Start a new topic by using a polite transition like, "That may be, but did you know...?" Move right into your next topic like this:

Speaker: "I can't believe the boss got on her case for doing that ..."

You: "Yeah, he can be tough, but have you seen the new computers he bought?"

Describe personal features. Describe the physical and personal you as part of an ongoing discussion or by starting a new discussion. Tell the listeners something *positive about yourself.* Positive attributes should be visible at the time so you can generate complimentary reactions. Say something like, "Hey guys, did you notice my new briefcase. I really like it."

"But wait a minute! That sounds like bragging. I can't do that!" Yes, you can. You're not bragging. You're describing something you like about yourself and that pertains to the situation. You're proud of something, and you're just sharing your pride with other people. Braggarts never share their pride. They just announce why they're better than other people. You're not saying you're better. You're saying you have something you like. And you are entitled to like things and let others know your taste.

Solicit personal compliments. It's one thing to tell somebody something. It's another to ask him or her for an opinion on it. That's what soliciting personal compliments is all about. You make a conspicuous effort to be asked about, wear, or show some personal characteristic or item. Maybe it's a particular outfit you really like. For some it's their political views. You prompt the exercise by saying, "What do you think about ..."

Good replies are accepted with "Thank you." Unfavorable replies receive the same response: "Thank you." You're not taking a poll on your personality or some personal feature. All you want is experience putting your *self* up for auction and seeing the results. Whether it's good or bad is irrelevant. You just want an honest answer.

Accept compliments without discrediting them. It's no joke. Saying "Thank you" and leaving it at that is difficult. Overwhelmed by shame, you instantly feel compelled to apologize for looking good, smelling good, wearing nice clothing, or doing a good deed. Nothing ever seems good enough to deserve praise. Accepting praise feels like you're saying you're better than another person, and he or she will know it when you gobble up all the compliments. Better you should be humble, right?

Wrong. Fighting guilt head-on means a moratorium on humbleness. You can't afford to buy into old habits if you hope to really beat guilt. You beat guilt by trying strange new behaviors you envy in others, but dare not experience yourself. Now you can experience them. We'll take it step by step. Let's start with a general compliment:

Person: "My, you look beautiful in that outfit.
You: "Thank you."

DO NOT SAY:
- "Gee, it's just an old outfit."
- "Oh, you're just being kind, really it's nothing."
- "Oh, thanks, but your outfit looks better than mine."

- "Well, maybe, but you know nothing else looks good on me."

A simple *thank you* will do. Of course, the mercury goes up when compliments get more personal. Specific remarks about your physical shape or intelligence dig deep and may pinch an emotional nerve ending. But don't back away. The stranger you feel, the more important it is to be brave and stay on track with "Thank you." For example:

Person: "I can't believe how insightful you are. You really pegged that one long before the deal was made. My goodness you're a natural at negotiations."

You: "Thanks."

Add on to compliments without fear. You got passed the hard step just saying *thank you.* Now, go farther. This time, after you say *thank you,* make a few remarks that embellish what the person praised you for. You qualify yourself along the lines of what the person said. Remember, it's not bragging because the person *already* acknowledges these strengths in you and wants to hear more. All you're doing is rounding out the situation so she gets the full picture. Here's how to do it:

Person: "How in the world do you keep so slender?"

You: "Thanks for noticing. I work-out twice a week at a local club and watch my diet."

Intimate flattery gets more difficult because you may not trust what the person is saying to you. Does he have a hidden agenda? Possibly. But right now you're not playing psychologist. Don't be an analyst. Don't read into words, phrases and body language, and feel you must interrogate the person before accepting the compliment. Accept the compliment first, you can ask questions about your doubts later.

Like your physical looks. Why do you hate the way you look? Did you know that most people raised in troubled families think they're ugly? Both men and women can't stand themselves in the mirror. It's like looking the demon straight in the eyes. Why is this?

It may be that, as a child, (1) you never received praise for how you looked, just what you did or didn't do. Or, (2) you never received praise for your looks because your parents thought it would "go to your head," and you'd develop a big ego. Or, (3) you were sexually teased, misused, or abused and forced to keep it secret or else face shameful consequences. Or, (4) you were alienated by friends for looking so good. In teen years, they thought you were "snobby." In adult years, they were afraid of you. Or, (5) all intimate partners wanted from you was sex. Nobody ever cared to get to know you. You hated their lust and felt angry at yourself for having caused it. Or, (6) you were embarrassed, ashamed or humiliated by the way people showered you with fake praise, sexual overtures, and hollow promises. Or, (7) you envied people less attractive than you who never faced these problems.

Attractive people suffer from *the impostor syndrome* because they can't imagine normal, healthy praise for their physical attributes. That is why when somebody says to you, "You should be a model," your first instinct is to think: "Why, so you can drool over me?" Your next thought, depending on your childhood experiences, either is to punch the daylights out of him or run home, take a long shower, and wash away the *dirty* feeling you get from their attraction.

But wait a minute. Just because other people can't handle your good looks doesn't mean you can't. What they can't handle is their problem, not yours. They envy you. You're special. Accept that special gift rather than trying vigorously to destroy it. You have naturally what so many people work hours in front of a mirror trying to produce. Some even undergo surgery hoping for a beautiful image. Your image is already there, and has been there for a long time. It's part of you. You can't get rid of it; and you don't want to.

To train yourself to accept the idea that it's okay to be attractive, look at yourself in the mirror every morning and briefly praise four of your physical attributes. Use four new attributes each day. DO NOT insult any part of your body during this exercise.

Using the *soliciting approach* discussed earlier, ask a person close to you about a physical characteristic you've noticed in the mirror. Ask the question in a positive way, such as "Don't you think my mustache looks good?" Remember to thank the person for agreeing with your statement. Then embellish the person's positive remarks.

Wear makeup or get a hairstyle that complements your attractive features. Never hide your beauty. It's easy to hide your nice figure or looks by not wearing make-up, getting your hair or nails done, or having body odor. "Hah, that will keep people away from me!" Wrong. You've got it backward. That will keep you away from other people. And it will keep you away from the people you want close to you. So, change this game plan by getting a facial, changing your hairdo, and caring about your hygiene.

The same is true of clothing. Choose clothing that accentuates your figure. Sure, bright colors draw attention and slim-fitting items may bring unwanted flattery from onlookers. So what? That's what you want.

"NO," you say, "it's not! That's what somebody did to me when I was young and I hated him and I hated myself for allowing that to happen."

Okay, calm down. That was then. This is now. Years ago those who teased, misused, and abused you spoiled a good thing. They made you feel ashamed of compliments about how you look. But compliments are normal. Think of them like pizza. If you took a lot of flack for eating pizza as a teen, you may hate pizza today and think anybody who eats it or talks about it is a creep. Fine. But, most American adults enjoy eating pizza. They talk about pizza, they look for pizza restaurants, and pizza is a national household word. It's normal to like pizza.

You're the one who has the problem, not the pizza-lovers. You need to break through that wall of pizza-hatred to enjoy a part of life you have denied yourself because of childhood fears. And that's what pizza has in common with your appearance. You can't fear your looks forever. Whatever happened is done with. Let it go. Open the window and smell the fresh air. It's out there waiting for you to smell it. And once you do that, you will see that you can be proud of being attractive. This will make you feel sad and angry. Sad that you waited so long to recapture something snatched from you years ago. And angry, because you'll want to defend your right to be attractive, and never let it be taken away again.

Reversing the Impostor Situation

You must always try to overcome obstacles—despite the odds. And the impostor inside you must fight the odds so that you can feel genuine. That is why you need to reverse the impostor situation. Reversing it sounds complicated. But it's not. You simply take the following steps when that impostor feeling overwhelms you in a situation.

Stay in the situation. Don't go anywhere. No avoidance and escape allowed. Remain seated, standing, or wherever you are at the time the impostor feeling hits. Continue your conversation. Breathe naturally as you talk.

Ask questions focused on other people. Staying stationary is hard enough. Now you need to start your motor. Add energy to the situation. Ask questions about things you're not sure about. Give opinions you think are open to attack. Be animated with your speech so it distracts you from monitoring your every move. You feel like you're watching yourself on a closed-circuit television program. You can escape that feeling by enthusiastically participating in a conversation. Immerse yourself in the dialogue, laughter, or debate.

DO NOT just sit back and listen. Listening may be polite and guarantee others will approve of you, but it also lets you scan everything you're doing. Forget it. Be a participant, not part of the camera crew.

Adjust body language. Physically step into the situation. Close the physical distance between you and another person. Walk up to her. Shake her hand. Sit next to her at a meeting. Closeness (not intimate closeness) blocks self-monitoring. You become so attuned to the person inches away from you that you aren't overly concerned with your own actions.

Stop-technique. Okay, so the above methods are working fine. But you still have intrusive thoughts—"Who are you kidding? You're just a joke. They all know it, too." These thoughts build to a peak, scaring you to death and making you feel ashamed. So, you need to stop them. Say *stop* to yourself. Then immediately shift your attention to what others are talking about, or join the conversation. Use the *stop-interruption* every time your old fears slip up on you.

Say good-bye to being scared, and to feeling like an impostor. You never wanted to feel that way. And the people who made you feel that way are probably not as important to you anymore. If they still are, you're learning to deal with them so you can put the impostor feeling to sleep forever. You now know it's okay to do things wrong; say things wrong; make stupid mistakes; and feel embarrassed. Failure is a part of life for all of us. It's not evil. It just happens. So, join the club.

STEP 7
No More Toxic Shame

Time-out. You've had a chance to practice some new skills and get a feeling for this guilt-free world. You know it's out there—you can see it, taste it, and almost grasp it in your hands. You're on the verge of holding on to it. You're inches away. It's that close.

So what's making it slip out of your hands? Why can't you get rid of guilt forever? You know the answer, don't you? It's that chilling feeling of being *no good*. You can sit on it, ignore it, and pretend it's not there. But it is. That inner voice keeps telling you to admit defeat. That voice saying you're no good and everything is your fault. It's like a thorn in your side. Even when you take the thorn out you still feel the lasting pain of its wound. So, you have to deal with that phantom pain. The pain of feeling guilty even when you're not guilty of anything.

Step 7 will help you learn when it's okay to be wrong, bad, defiant, and independent. These things are not taboo anymore. You can may these choices, but you need to check them out first.

When Is It Okay to Be Wrong?

Wrong is your nickname. You got it early in childhood and now it follows you around. No matter how daring you are, how far you leap into the fire, later on you still harp on how wrong it was to do those things. And why? It is because doing things wrong means people will dislike you and you'll be left all alone.

WRONG = DISAPPROVAL + LONELINESS

Is there a way to break this cycle? Yes. To help you puncture the tightly-sealed bubble of fear found in most close relationships, here are some suggestions.

In friendships. Friends are those who do things for *you,* rather than your always being the one doing things for them. Take steps to allow yourself to be wrong by deliberately charting new territory.

- Refuse to do things you usually do for someone.
- Ask someone to do things for you without giving something in return.
- Be angry at your friend, or blame him for some-thing.
- Let your friend be upset, inconvenienced, or put through grief.
- Break a promise or commitment, or change some scheduled plan.
- Make new friends, even if you feel it will jeopardize an old friendship.

Following these suggestions gives you permission to make mistakes with friends. It is okay to be bad or when you make new friends and leave old ones hanging; try new things without having friends help you; disagree with friends even when they seem right about something.

In intimate relationships. Closeness heats up shame. The closer you are with somebody—boyfriend, girlfriend, or platonic friend—the more you begin treating this person like you did people in your family—your father, mother or siblings. And once sexual intimacy enters the picture, shame gets stronger. You are especially sensitive around a sexual partner. All your efforts are focused on making this person feel good, and not being bad or wrong. You fear that spoiling this relationship will feel as wrong as having your family abandoning you. So, you do everything not to spoil the relationship.

But, of course, that causes more problems in the relationship. It's okay to be wrong in intimate relationships when you:

1. Say things your partner doesn't like to hear.

2. Go places your partner *forbids* you to go.
3. Socialize with friends your partner dislikes.
4. Insist your partner go places with you that he or she thinks are weird, childish, or just plain dumb.
5. Refuse having sex when you don't want sex. This means saying *no* to experimental sex, if what's being asked of you feels very strange or you know your partner's motivations are not romantic.
6. Let your partner be angry at you. You're not a fireman. You don't have to put out all of the fires of conflict in the relationship.
7. You can tell others about problems in your relationship. It's not a secret. Let the cat out of the bag if telling close friends or family makes you feel better. You're not "airing your dirty laundry." All you're doing is seeking advice and comfort from caring people.

In marriage. Once intimacy becomes marriage, fears of doing wrong turn from bad to worse. Now you're not just *feeling* like you're back home with Mom and Dad, you've actually *duplicated* the situation. You've done it once, and now you're doing it all over again—lock, stock, and barrel. Marriage suddenly means you cannot, should not, and better not violate certain "rules." You MUST:
1. keep your partner happy
2. keep the family unit intact
3. be friendly to your partner's family
4. live up to your partner's expectations
5. concede to your partner's wants and needs
6. keep all family matters private
7. regard your needs second and your partner's first

All these MUSTs protect you from feeling toxic shame. They protect you from doing the wrong thing and ending up paying emotional penalties later. But what is the worst thing that can happen to you?

Will your partner:
- yell at you?
- tease you?

- deny you money?
- have an affair?
- hit you?
- tell the kids you're bad?
- deny you sex?

Fine, these are all scary things. But, if they are real possibilities, don't they already happen to you anyway? So what do you have to lose? What's to be lost by a different approach when the aces seem to be are stacked against you. You think you're defeated, trapped, and that forcing more grief upon your spouse will only backfire; it makes your situation all the more difficult—if you give in to guilt.

When you surrender to feeling wrong and thinking you're a bad person, you become pessimistic; if something rotten can happen, it will happen. But you can reverse this attitude by breaking feelings of "wrong."

To do this, argue with your spouse. Always express you opinions. Always express your feelings. Insist that your spouse do things your way every other time. And, never grow too dependent on your spouse. If you think it's too late, because you don't have a job and you're stuck there with the kids, find a creative way to do things on your own. Think about more school. Think about a part-time job. Never sell your soul to the spouse-devil.

Also, let yours kids see you and your spouse argue. Arguing is not bad. It is a healthy sign of adult feelings. Children who see their parents exchange opinions begin to think of conflict as normal in families. As they grow up, and in their adult lives, they'll never be afraid of conflict and are more likely to marry a spouse who speaks up and doesn't stuff problems inside.

Tell your in-laws your personal opinions. Don't stand on ceremony with your spouse's family. Making a good impression after you marry is not necessary. Now is the time to build a lifelong rapport. Do it with honest feelings. Say what you like, dislike, and what you want them to do differently. Cause them temporary grief if you have to—but don't lie. Don't pretend that everything is okay when it isn't. You'll be sorry.

Be honest about your spouse to other people. Resist the temptation to exaggerate your spouse's positive personality traits. No more rosy pictures. Tell the truth about your spouse's good qualities, and be honest about the bad qualities. It's hard to do this, because saying bad things about your spouse makes *you* look bad. You think you're as good as your spouse is. So, if your spouse is no good, that's how you feel about yourself. That's why you pump up his or her image. That's why you tell white-lies. You look good because your spouse looks good. But you are a good person with or without your spouse.

And forget about making excuses for your spouse. You'll no longer do that. People get only the truth. If the boss calls and asks where he is, you tell him you don't know if you don't know. But, never say "I don't know" if you do know.

Break away from your spouse's unhealthy routines. If he steals, cheats, lies, drinks too much, overeats, or does things you didn't do before your relationship began, or you want to make changes for personal reasons, stop the offending behavior and let your spouse ruin his or her own life. You don't have to sink along with him. Just say, "No. I'm sorry, I'm not doing that with you anymore."

In sibling relationships. Siblings are your closest allies. They know what you're going through. You share childhood experiences. You share adult experiences. Part of you is part of them. They may even look like you, and behave like you, too. Even step-siblings are tied by emotional strings. You know them inside and out, and they say they can see through you. You know about their past, and they know about yours.

That's why you can't fool them. Your spouse—sure, you can do it. Your friends—sure, that's a piece of cake. But not siblings. No way, no how. You feel that any change you make throws up a red flag and they'll wonder what you're doing. So that's why you have to be direct. You'll have to tell them, (1) you're trying to be a different person; (2) you're enjoying the new *you*; (3) you're going to say and do things in a new way.

Recruiting your siblings into this 10-step program is a good idea if you feel close to them. They can help you monitor progress and keep you headed in the right direction. To help, supportive siblings need to be involved; don't ignore them or make them feel unwanted.

But, some siblings may not be your buddies. Maybe you haven't seen them for many years. Or, if you do see them, maybe it's hard to communicate with them. For one reason or another, you don't get along. That's why they can't be part of your 10-step program. Only enlist those siblings you talk to regularly and who really care about you.

In relationships with your mother and father. Now the hardest test of all—letting yourself be bad or wrong in front of the Spanish Inquisitors—the people who made you feel guilty in the first place. That's tough. And if you had your druthers, you'd really prefer to do something else. Facing your parents head-on is not your cup of tea. Or is it? Here's how you can break the taboos:

1. Disagree with things your parents say.
2. Tell them what you want them to do. That means you take control instead of being a servant to their commands. For example, suppose you plan to go to a restaurant with your folks for dinner. Fine: you choose the restaurant.
3. Resist advice they give you about what's right and what's wrong.
4. Deliberately wear clothing you like and not what they like. Your parents may expect you to look like a million dollars, for example. Surprise them, dress like a slob. But only if you *want* to. Never do anything just to spite your parents. It's the same with keeping your house clean. You might go crazy perfecting your house so it looks like a showcase before your parents arrive. Forget it. Let it look natural. Forced effort to please them only upsets you later.
5. Arrange to be with your parents individually. Never take them on as a team. One-on-one, be yourself. Express personal views and wants, and find fault with your parent.

If your parent is unhappy, let it be. It's okay for parents to be unhappy. They'll still love you, even if they say they don't.

6. Choose which parent is more critical. That's the parent you're afraid to do wrong things around. Chances are that your parents had opposite personalities. One parent was quieter, more compassionate, even saintly. Another was louder, more critical, and frequently angry. Both of your parents could have been this way. And possibly neither of them were until they drank alcohol. So which parent was it, Dad or Mom? Choose the parent who is tougher to deal with, and take your risks with that parent. Being bad or wrong with your parents is a great achievement. You've finally broken the barrier; you are no longer trapped in childhood memories; you no longer have to be a little kid around them. You're above that now. You're stronger, braver, and really want to be treated like their equal—which you are.

In parent-child relationships. What about your kids? Sure, you love them. Sure, you'd do anything for them. You live for their survival. But can you be yourself around them? Are you too afraid to be wrong in front of them? You shouldn't be. They're fresh for learning. Let them absorb the new you so they can learn how to beat guilt in their early years. There are many possibilities.

1. Make mistakes in front of them.
2. Tell them their mistakes are *okay* and laugh with them about some of the mistakes.
3. Show your children new things you're trying. If it's baking a cake for the first time, let them watch you and see your failures. If it's laying a new lawn on your own, let the kids work with you. Let them *participate in your risk-taking behavior so they learn early on that it's okay to make mistakes.*
4. Encourage them to try new things their friends don't do. Tell them that *different is good. You're better off and*

usually more popular by being yourself than by copying other people.

When Is It Okay To Be Bad?

While *wrong* is deviant, *bad* is downright nasty. That's how you'll feel. You feel awful. You're not towing the line. You're not doing and saying what you're supposed to. And something bad is going to happen. You just know it will. That's why you think *you're* bad. If something bad might happen, it's because you caused it. So, you're the bad person.

Is there any time that being bad is okay? Sure, if you want to be a guilt-fighter. Guilt-fighters *want* to be bad. This is what being BAD means.

1. You do the opposite of what people expect.
2. You try things people think you can't do.
3. You break the customs or rules of some establishment: a family or business, the church.
4. You draw people into the *bad* things you do.
5. You go against your natural instinct to escape.

At work. Can you be bad at work? Sometimes you want to be bad but you can't accept the risks. You think you'll be fired. The risk is too great, the benefits too remote. So, you repeat your daily routines and feel more and more suffocated by the pressure. The pressure of others making you do more work. You do work that they won't do. You do work that they can't do. You do your bosses' work, and you do your co-workers' work. You step in where you're needed. And the funny thing is, you seem to be needed everywhere you turn.

The way to be bad at work is to violate your personal rules of conduct. Here are a few ways to go about this.

1. Don't be so eager to help people in distress. Either let them help themselves, or guide their efforts instead of doing everything for them.
2. Don't stay late to work. Go home at quitting time. If you're going to stay late, be paid for it.

3. Don't work through your breaks. You're entitled by law to three breaks. One in the morning, one for lunch, and one in the afternoon. Plan to use them all.

4. Slow your pace down. Work at a somfortable, consistent speed.

"I can't do that. People rely on me!" That's right, they do. But, sometimes supervisors and fellow employees rely on you to do more than your fair share, while they work at an unharried, comfortable pace. They're used to your working fast, working hard, and craving more work. They know you're a workaholic. So they flatter you; they tell you that you'll be getting a raise. They bring you treats and tell people how efficient you are.

And you bite the bait. You go for their oo-ing and aah-ing because it feels good for somebody to finally approve of you. But they're not really approving of you; they don't really think you are so wonderful. They think you are a *sucker*. They want to keep you right where you are: no raise, no promotion, no transfer. They want to keep things status quo. And why? Because if you leave, then they have to work harder. They have to do things they don't know how to do. Things you've always done for them. Your leaving will expose how inept they really are. And they won't let that happen. So, you're there for keeps.

You do more for more people because you feel guilty. So, you can stop the cycle by refusing to be a workaholic.

To achieve this you reduce your daily effort so that it takes you longer to finish what you used to do in minutes. Next, you extend your deadlines instead of promising to get things done in a flash. Don't try to do everything yourself, and tell supervisors things take longer than expected. Finally, this will force your boss to realize you can't do all the work alone. Your boss will see by your slower pace that more help is needed in the office.

No matter how many times you complain about being overworked and underpaid, none of your complaints will mean anything until the boss is inconvenienced. When the boss feels the effects of your slow-down, suddenly his or her eyes open and action is taken.

When Is It Okay to Be Defiant?

You probably believe defiance is never okay, right? That's only true if you think *defiance* is a vulgar word. But it's not. It's something most people do all the time. They do it a little at a time. Being defiant means *taking risks*. You can take minor risks, and it won't lead you to destruction. You won't become a thief. You won't become a liar. You won't become a murderer. And you won't become so immoral or unethical that you can't stand yourself. None of this will ever happen.

Do you know why? It's because you won't allow yourself to be very defiant. You have a built-in alarm clock that goes off if you start going over the edge. That alarm clocks rings so loudly that you stop dead in your tracks and can't move. It stifles you.

But the good news is that this alarm clock is trigger-happy. In the past it's gone off for minor violations. Talking back, doing things behind a person's back, talking about yourself—all of these things set off the alarm. Your alarm didn't let you get away with anything. So, now you're re-setting the alarm. You're letting yourself get away with much more before the alarm rings. You try to give yourself a lot of latitude. You try to do more daring things before the alarm warns you of danger.

There's only one problem. No matter how liberal you are, that alarm will still go off too early. You'll never permit yourself heavy-duty risk-taking before that alarm rings. It's in you to be safe. You may conquer guilt, but you'll always keep yourself safe.

That's why you'll be defiant in a very different way. It will never be like other people. For you, defiance is only an approximation. It's a step toward really being defiant. You'll never do anything that's off the wall. You simply can't be *totally* awful.

So how defiant can you be? That's what you will find out in this section. Here are some ways to be defiant in your marriage or in relationships, and in your creativity.

In your marriage or relationships. Imagine the altar where you were married. Now insert a new film in that image. Imagine yourself stepping up to the altar and shouting, "No way, I won't marry this creep!" Funny, eh? You can laugh at it because you're thinking, "I'd never really do that, but boy it's nice to think about." It's nice to imagine being rude, crude, and trashy. Just picture yourself going off the deep end. You swear at your spouse and all of his family. The picture gets even sweeter when you imagine yourself in charge of everything. You give the orders. No more Mr. Nice Guy. You're the head honcho. You say *jump,* and your spouse jumps. Picture it. It feels good, doesn't it?

Is it only a fantasy? No. These mental images can be real. They do not have to remain fantasy. Step outside your imagination for a moment and ask yourself, "How can I do what I'd really like to do?"

- How can I be selfish? How can I spend money on just me?
- How can I get my way more often? How can I be the one in charge of what we do, or who we see?
- How can I make a career move or take a leap of faith in a new   direction? How can I *just do this* without ruining the marriage?
- How can I be healthier? How can I exercise more, and stop my smoking, drinking, or overeating?
- How can I become happy? Who do I need to see or what decisions do I need to make that will tip over this boring life so that it crashes to the ground? Then I'll be forced to start it all over again, this time taping the pieces of my life together in a healthier way.

You can answer these questions if you do the following:

1. Take an inventory of what you want out of your life.
2. Make a list of those things you wish you could be or do. Do it now.

I WISH I COULD:

a. _____   e.g., be more physically fit.

b. _____

c. _____

3. Now, break down each item you listed, into smaller segments. These segments tell you how to go about accomplishing your goals. For example:

be more physically fit

> join a club
> save money for it
> start with daily exercise

a. _____

> (a)_____
> (b)_____
> (c)_____

b. _____

> (a)_____
> (b)_____
> (c)_____

c. _____

> (a)_____
> (b)_____
> (c)_____

4. Plan on working through these steps. Make them your daily obsession. Try to reach your goal by completing each step.

In your creativity. Your private world is the easiest world for defiance. Usually your thoughts are on guard duty, checking your every move and guessing what people think of them. But not anymore. Now you can use your mind for creativity. Turn your analyzing energy into an art form, make it explore new abilities in you that seem strange and impossible. Reach deep into your mind's eye and pull out an idea for a project.

Suppose the project is to read a book. You rarely read books, but now is the time to start. You don't just want to read your everyday, garden-variety books. You're interested in a very different type. A book on fantasy, on hobbies, on consumer buying, or on history—on any topic you've never really thought about, let alone read about. Except now these types of books hold your interest. They tap a hidden passion for information.

You want to feed this passion. Okay—go buy the book. Buy two or three of them.

Enrich your creativity by coming up with off-the-wall ideas that go against what you usually think about during the day. Not only think about these ideas, but act on them. Follow through on your creative thoughts. You won't be disappointed; you won't get hurt, either. You'll feel exhilarated—a load has been lifted off your shoulders. You've just discovered a new way of thinking. Thinking that says you can do anything, if you only try.

The extent to which a creative idea succeeds or fails is less important than *acting on it*. Acting on your ideas lets you trust yourself; you begin to perceive of yourself as a think-tank, capable of troubleshooting problems, making decisions, and living more fully. You become your own psychologist. You begin to depend on yourself for getting out of messes. You learn to say, "I can do it myself." And what's more, you really do work through problems without caring about others.

When Is It Okay to Be Independent?

You want *out*. You want out because you hate being dependent on somebody else. You feel like a prisoner refused parole. And worst of all—you're the parole board who's saying, "Stay put, don't move." You do this so you don't:

- abandon the person
- cause the person grief
- blame yourself for not handling things or running away
- feel selfish

Each step you take toward becoming independent is a step farther from the comfort zone. The comfort zone is that imaginary boundary around your life and your partner's life. You believe you belong inside that boundary. You dare not cross over the line. You don't even dare to think about doing it. Crossing over the line constitutes a violation. You believe your partner will hate you for doing it. Or that something bad—you know not what—will happen.

Consider:

Jackie—she stayed at home, raised three kids and never did volunteer work because she thought her husband would hate her "sharing her time."

Bruce—he worked at a boring state government job, even though he wanted to try opening up an auto shop. He was afraid his wife would think he was irresponsible and leave him.

Regina—she never drove a car. She had her driver's license, but she couldn't bear her husband's badgering. He'd always ask where she was going. He'd check the gas gauge and odometer. His paranoia was too much to handle.

Rick—he lived at home with his parents. He worked all day, but that's all he did. His mother made him her own personal slave. Whatever she wanted, he did. He had to do it. He was to afraid not to do it.

All of these people share a common fear. "Don't trespass across the boundary or you'll pay nasty consequences for it." They internalized this fear so deeply they wouldn't budge. That's how you feel. You want to start something new—you even know you can do it—but you won't attempt it for fear of being: teased—yelled at—denied privileges—belittled—threatened—deprived of money and affection—physically hurt—abandoned.

And the honest truth is, you don't deserve any of these nasty things. But they may happen, because the person you depend on is also dependent on you. That's what is meant by *codependent.* You need this person for security as much as this person desperately draws oxygen out of you for survival. It's a two-way—defective—street.

You can begin to break the codependency trap in a relationship or friendship by violating the boundary. You must step over the boundary and into a refreshing world of selfish pride, full of personal awareness and happiness. A world where you can take credit for things you do and not watch others take your credit away. A world where you can be creative and imaginative, and let your inhibitions go without worrying who'll hurt you. In this world you can take risks and defeat toxic shame in three ways.

First, try things literally opposite to what you've been allowed to do or think. Be radical. Join an organization, show interest in new religions, or be more social. Try looking into activities, events, and groups you previously dismissed as *bad* or *taboo.*

Second, become another person by copying the good features of a person you admire. When you start, think like that person. You won't always be a carbon-copy. Only at first; only during the first weeks. That's when you experiment with acting like they do. After the first week you'll begin to merge their ways with your own personality. Then you'll become a new *you.*

Third, try doing something new or difficult by yourself. Bust out of the boundary bubble not only by being different and copying things risky people do, but by trying these things entirely on your own. Don't ask somebody to be your coach. You don't need one. You must try it alone. You must experience the trials and tribulations of fumbling, stumbling, and rambling. You must dance around in circles, thinking you're going nowhere and feeling worried that nothing you're doing will really work.

It Is Important to Go Through These Steps.

Part of independence is the discovery period. You'll discover that mistakes you make are humiliating, stupid, and aggravating. But mistakes are necessary. You must go through the frightening self-doubts involved in taking risks before you'll feel okay on the other side of the boundary.

Boundaries, like rules, are made to be broken. Once you step over the boundary, it disappears. No longer is there a boundary separating you from the pleasures of the rest of your life. You are free to choose your own direction and weather life's little storms along the way.

STEP 8
No More Need for Control

Did you ever go to a friend's party? You're there to have a good time, but you notice your friends struggling: too many dishes, too much to clean up, and too many people. It looks overwhelming. You don't think they can handle it. You feel sorry for them. After all, they are your friends, right?

So you decide to help out. You pick up the dishes. You take out the trash. You carry the pizza tray around. You even suggest when it's time to serve dessert. They didn't ask you to do it. You just did it on your own. You're there to help. You'd like it if they did it for you, so why wouldn't they like it if you did it for them? After all, that's what friends are for. Isn't that right?

WRONG. That's how you lose friends. Nobody asked you to pitch in, so why did you do it? Why didn't you mind your own business?

"Mind my own business? But I was just trying to help, wasn't I?"

NO. Not in your friend's eyes. And not according to many people who dislike helpers. They dislike helpers because they think the helper is saying they can't do something well. They want to be in control, and you stole that away from them. They have a problem with control. And so do you.

This chapter is about control. Control can make or break friendships. It can create and ruin relationships. And it can build up your hopes and expectations only to have them smashed. All due to trying too hard to be what nobody wants you to be—a helper.

And why? Because you're not really helping: you're controlling. You're at that party cleaning up so that things will go smoothly. But for whom? Your friend or yourself? Your friend may be going crazy, but maybe that's how he likes doing things. Your friend may find things get done—right or wrong—by jumping around and looking anxious. That's their modus operandi—their standing operational procedure. That's how they've done it in the past. That's how they're doing it now. And that's how they'll probably do it at their next party. It's just their way of doing things.

You mix in because you don't do things like that. You couldn't. It's too chaotic. You look at their behavior and say, "My God, if I felt like that I'd be going nuts. " You think you'd want help, so they probably want help.

But your friends never asked for your help, and you gave it anyway. You pitched in to organize your friends' world the way you feel comfortable with it. You controlled your friends' environment so that you could relieve your own anxiety. It was bothering you to watch them looking tense. You felt nervous and ashamed, and thought your way would solve the problem.

Nobody asked for your help. Nobody wanted you to intervene. And now, nobody appreciates what you've done.

That's the sickening consequence of needing to control things. You can't win at it. Just when you think you're saving people from disaster, you're really creating the disaster for them. Control never benefits the person. Either it robs them of feeling control or it makes them so dependent on you that they always want you to be in control. There's no middle ground. You always lose.

Control is not a benevolent act. You think it is, however. You think you're doing things to make people happy, but you're not. You're actually doing good things to protect yourself from bad things. Control acts as protection against all the fears you have about what people will say or do to you. By taking charge, you can make sure these bad things never pop up at the moment. And should they pop up later, you can blame the other person for being too selfish and not appreciating your generous efforts. Of course, this still all boils down to *you protecting yourself to avoid feeling shame.*

Why Controlling Is Really Protecting

Shame plays dirty tricks on you. One of them is being on the look-out for conflict and grief. You don't like conflict and you won't deliberately cause a person grief. So, you stick your nose into situations to reduce the risk of conflict and grief. You're protecting yourself like a guard protects a house. You won't let anything you don't authorize get in under your nose. You can't. It would be too awful. You protect against anything and anyone that threatens your vulnerability. You won't look stupid—you refuse!

What exactly are these threats you protect against? And how can you break the barriers of protection for each one? Let's take a look.

Protecting yourself from criticism and conflict. There's nothing you can do that won't upset somebody. Angry people pop up everywhere, blaming you for incredible wrongs they want you to believe you did. And you used to believe them. They sounded convincing. Take, for instance, "You're so self-centered."

It's a common complaint. But now the thinking begins. "Maybe they're right for saying this about me." You instantly review the day's events—things you said and did. You figure you were selfish once or twice. "Yea, I suppose I did buy that CD player for myself ... and, I guess I did eat the snacks we saved for the family." That's the evidence. You've been caught. You're in trouble now. This evidence is all it takes to indict yourself. You're guilty. Forget how selfish the person criticizing you is; forget the fact that everybody does self-centered things every day anyway. All that matters is that what the critical person said hit the nail on the head. And one nail and one head is all it takes. Any shred of evidence of self-centered behavior automatically implicates you.

"By God, they're right! I am self-centered." It's that fast. You accept the verdict without considering why this person is critical and whether you really deserve the guilt. It doesn't matter. You're at fault and you feel trapped, unable to squirm out of it. You try to escape criticism and conflict by agreeing, apologizing, defending yourself, blaming yourself, even going overboard to please the other person. You also blow up at, argue with, or walk away from the person criticizing you. If that doesn't work, you might get angrier and raise your fists or throw nearby objects.

Failing at hostility, you're not through yet. You have other protective tricks up your sleeve. After the onslaught of criticism, you'll practically do anything to prevent the ensuing conflict. This means interrupting the argument to call friends and family for their support. You want their confirmation. You want them to confirm you're a good person inside and that nothing the critical person said is really true. No way, no how. That person is wrong on all accounts.

You also use *make-me-feel-good tactics* to protect yourself from conflict. When you feel defeated by a criticism, rather than talk back to the critic, you go out and spend money you don't have; you eat more than usual; you drink more liquor than usual. Your make-me-feel-good tactics go into motion. Married spouses start flirting with the opposite sex. Employed spouses go on more business trips. Family outings decline rapidly. You start to perceive of yourself as alone in this awful struggle to be appreciated. Nobody loves you or wants you, and you feel like you're fighting an uphill battle for self-esteem. You have to look out for yourself, because nobody else will.

This is a self-centered distortion. You're really not alone. You're really not under-appreciated. And you certainly are not fighting an uphill battle for self-esteem. There is no battle, because there is no enemy. You're the only enemy attacking here; you're attacking yourself. All the other person did is to make a negative comment about you. Right or wrong, that comment is just a comment. It's not a ...

1. Commandment: "Thou art bad. You should be ashamed";
2. Diagnosis: "You have a serious disorder and will never get better";
3. Verdict: "You committed a heinous crime and deserve the death penalty";
4. Rule: "You always do these things wrong and you'll never do them right."

You shift into the *protect-me gear* because you honestly believe that criticism is one or all of these four things. So that's the first thing to change. Change how you look at criticism and conflict. Regard criticism as (1) normal, (2) a bunch of words, (3) something the person wants but isn't getting, (4) something you want but are trying to get the wrong way, (5) a statement of concern from somebody who cares about you, or (6) a statement about how somebody wants to help you.

Nobody criticizes you if they think you're unimportant. No matter how harsh the words, criticism is always a helping gesture.

Conflict works the same way. Some people think conflict is arguing, and arguments are bad in relationships. Arguing, they think, signals poor communication and an outright struggle for control. But that's not so. Arguments are words, but they are also helping gestures. In fact, many benefits come from conflict and arguments. Here are just some of the possible benefits.

- You say what's on your mind.
- You relieve pent-up tensions.
- You hear what another person is thinking.
- You learn more facts about a situation.
- You listen to solutions to a problem.

Conflict is only scary if you listen to those internal messages that say you're losing control and don't want to be bullied by another person. That's a distorted perception. That's looking at conflict as if it is a commandment, diagnosis, verdict, or rule. This kind of thinking suggests that you are under siege and running out of ammunition. You don't want to bail out and you're tired of fighting. So what's left to do?

How about staying right where you are? Don't flee. Don't take the offensive. Just face up to criticism and conflict as if talking in a normal conversation. That's all criticism and conflict are: opinions in a discussion. Criticism and conflict are not the enemy—they're your window into the world of friends, family, and intimate relationships. You get an inside view of their perceptions of you. That's why it's time to lift the protective veil from your emotions and embrace conflict and criticism. Here's how to do it.

How not to protect it. Get out of the "I don't want conflict and criticism" trap by following five guidelines:

GUIDELINE 1: Always stay *in* the situation.

GUIDELINE 2: Listen to what the person is saying before responding.

GUIDELINE 3: Never take criticism and conflict personally. Just ask what the person is saying, not why he or she is saying it.

GUIDELINE 4: Use the DESC method of assertiveness to speak your mind.

GUIDELINE 5: Use special relaxation methods to remain calm, so you won't flee from fear.

Protecting Yourself from Rejection

"He did it to me again. Why do I let him do this to me? I should have spotted the warning signs. But I didn't. I'm so stupid. I'll never learn ..." Learn what? Learn to take wiser precautions? Learn to jump the gun even faster, way before knowing the facts? Are you doing this just to avoid feeling hated? Will it really get you anywhere?

No, it won't. You feel miserable when you feel hated. But it isn't the hate somebody has for you that is making you feel miserable. Your misery comes from feeling disappointed. That's what rejection is: blaming yourself for feeling disappointed. For example, your girlfriend says she's going out tonight with her friends: you feel rejected. Your husband turns on the TV and turns into a couch potato: you feel rejected. Your best friend apologetically says she's can't go to the movie with you: you feel rejected.

But who's rejecting who? Is it your boyfriend's fault? Is it your girlfriend's fault? How about your spouse's or best friend's fault? Maybe it feels right blaming them. But that's not who's making you feel rejected. The fault lies with you. You're rejecting yourself. You're not handling a disappointment.

You don't like things not going your way. It's not because you're selfish, but because you depend so heavily on people making you feel worthwhile that if they say, "sorry, can't make it," it translates into "sorry, you're a jerk." You think disappointment means:

- "Nobody loves me or ever will."
- "Everybody takes me for granted."
- "They don't want me because I did something wrong to them."
- "I don't deserve people doing things with me. And people saying *no* to me proves they really don't want me."

Hating yourself for being rejected diverts you from the real issue: the fact that somebody can't or won't do something with you or for you. You forget the obvious. It vanishes into thin air. Your only concern is why they're doing it and what you should have done to prevent being put in this situation. That's what leads you to protecting yourself from rejection. And you protect yourself by:

- not asking people to do things with you.
- not letting people help you.
- not asking opinions about things you like.
- not asking people to do too much for you so you don't have to *owe* them.

You hate emotional debt. You'd rather scale the highest mountain using old gym shoes than ask someone to buy you climbing shoes and forever owe him a favor in return. It's just not worth building up an account with another person, because you feel you'll deposit more into it than they will. You'll always give more to somebody than you'll get in return.

But actually this is not true. You probably hate being indebted to others because it means you have to risk doing something for the person that they may dislike or reject. Or, the person may like your idea and may want your favor, but not exactly how you're giving it. And in your perception, that's no good. "Either I give it to the person the way I want to, or absolutely forget it. I won't change my idea or favor to please this person." And why? "Why should I? He won't like that either."

Already you've made a blueprint of rejection paths around your life. If it's not coming through one door, out it comes through another door—but sure enough, rejection is coming. You feel there is no avoiding this. You feel your life revolves around rejection. "People don't want me, and don't like me. They never will, and that's that." It's an open and shut case. That is, as long as you're keeping the blinders on. The blinders are distorting the real events.

Take the blinders off for a moment. Look at rejection differently. Think of rejection as an *opinion*. It's not a *judgment*. Nobody is deciding your fate. Nobody is deciding your decency as a human being. Opinions do the opposite. They're just reactions to what's going on. You have opinions just like everybody else. You're learning to express your opinion, so it makes sense that other people want to express their opinions. No opinion is right or wrong. It is only what the person feels at that moment. Accept it as an opinion for the moment. And let the person own that opinion. It belongs to him. He said it, he believes it, and he owns it. You don't own it, and there's no reason to take it seriously.

Think of rejection as:
- another person's opinion.
- another person's opinion that entirely belongs to that person.
- another person's opinion that may or may not deal with your ideas.
- another person's opinion that is neither true nor false, but just an opinion.

"Okay, fine. But I still hate that opinion. I still feel rejected by it." Don't feel rejected. Look at it as a benefit. There are many reasons to welcome other people's opinions.

1. You want people to be honest with you.

2. You want people to treat you fairly.

3. You want people to do what they feel *genuine* doing. You don't want them faking things just to make you happy.

4. You want people to respect you as a person.

5. You want the same kind of treatment you show to them.

So, it's okay for people to say things that make you feel rejected. You must experience rejection to realize people can't always pump up your ego, and so that you can recognize honesty when you are faced with it.

How not to protect it. Your greatest challenge in life is fighting shame when you feel rejected. But it's time to face facts. Take yourself off the disabled list of rejection for a moment. If you follow these guidelines, you'll learn to cope with life's many disappointments.

GUIDELINE 1: Thank someone for explaining why he did whatever made you feel rejected.

GUIDELINE 2: Say to yourself, "It's okay for a person to disappoint me. It just means that person can't do something with me or for me right now—not forever. And each of us has our own life. Everyone can't always do what I want when I want it. "

GUIDELINE 3: Ask people to do things for you and let yourself feel you *owe them.*

GUIDELINE 4: Do as much for people as they do for you— no more, no less. Don't build up a high tally of favors given and think the person now owes you plenty of favors in return. It won't work. It can't work; you're not giving the person a chance to give things back to you. Don't hog the favors. Let the other person scratch your back after you've scratched his.

Protecting Yourself from Anger

You hate getting angry. It's not "lady-like" or it's "too macho." Anger is a sign of weakness. That's how you feel. That's why holding in anger feels like you're in control. You call the shots. Let somebody else make a fool out of himself. Not you—no way. You're not losing your cool because things go awry.

But that's where the problem begins: repressing anger. You think it's more powerful, more in control. Trapping your frustrations inside stops you from outwardly acting like a maniac. You feel withholding or protecting your anger lets you (1) remain calm and in control, (2) appear strong and competent, (3) avoid conflict, criticism or rejection, (4) avoid looking vulnerable and as *bad* as the other person.

You can't imagine any good coming from showing your anger. But there are other reasons you protect your anger besides hating what it looks like. You won't get angry because: You don't know how to. It's one extreme or the other. You'll feel guilty after you do.

You don't know how to. Who doesn't know how to get mad? You just open your mouth and say bad things, right? It's so easy—in fact some people do it habitually and can't figure out why others take offense at it. Just the same, you might have grown up never hearing people argue. Your parents didn't argue. Your grandparents didn't argue. Your siblings, if you had any, rarely argued. It was a quiet household. The less said, the better things were. Sure, you still knew when your mother or father was angry at you—who wouldn't know? You could feel it in the air. There were no words, just a sense: a sixth sense. Nobody spoke in anger. So you inferred it. You knew when something was rotten and, after awhile, words wouldn't have made a difference anyway.

Growing up in a silent household robbed you of seeing conflict. You didn't see two people get mad; two people share opinions; two people lose their temper; and two people emotionally upset. None of this happened. It didn't happen then and it's not likely to happen now. This is because you don't know what anger feels like; even if you do feel it—and know it's anger— you only know one thing to do with it. You tuck it away like your parents and family did. That seems the normal thing to do.

Otherwise, watch out. Those funny sensations put a panic bug in you. "Oh, my God, what are these feelings I'm having?" It's anger but you might think it's something else—like a cold or a nervous breakdown. Your body is not used to twitching and tightening; your muscles feel pressure in them; your thoughts are spinning. And you might think you're losing your mind. It's a complete mental breakdown, or worse—you're becoming senile at a young age. "Now for sure nobody will want me."

It's one extreme or the other. "If I get angry, watch out— there'll be hell to pay." This is how you figure you'll react if you risk being angry the way you think people get angry. And where do you get your ideas of anger, if you've never done it yourself? How about from Mom or Dad or a close friend, or especially a girlfriend, boyfriend, or spouse? They blow at the slightest hint of conflict. And if that's the way to do it, beware world: "When I get pissed, it's nuclear explosion time." You'll swing from absolute passivity to outright aggression. There doesn't seem to be a middle of the road. It's either one or the other. As far as you know, this is the *only* way to get angry.

Of course, you can't stand seeing your parents, friends, or spouses get angry that way, so you certainly don't want to be angry like that yourself. Becoming that rowdy, that out of control is too frightening. So you do the safe thing. You protect your anger.

You'll feel guilty after you do. Another reason to tuck away anger is that it makes you hate yourself. You start ragging on yourself for doing the absolutely forbidden thing; you broke the life commandment that says, "Thou shall not lose thy temper against thy neighbors." You went a wrong way down a one-way street. You committed a cardinal sin and now must pay for it by condemning yourself for being so stupid. And here are some of the ways you blame yourself.

- You replay the anger-episode over and over in your mind to figure out how you could have said or done something differently.

- You deny yourself something you like or worked hard for as punishment for being bad.

- You do something that hurts or is bad for you, like using alcohol, cigarettes, marijuana, or other drugs, or doing something that is hard.

- You apologize to people you think you hurt or made enemies of. It doesn't matter if it was their fault; if you got angry, suddenly you're the only one to blame.

Guilty actions lead you down a path of self-doom because that's what you feel is right. Your parents did this to you; maybe your spouse or intimate does it to you; so, it feels right doing it to yourself. This doesn't mean you enjoy doing it or believe it's the best way of handling shameful feelings. But that doesn't matter. You fully intend to punish yourself for acting like a bad child.

How not to protect it. You don't need a license to get angry. You don't need to justify why it's right to be angry in one situation and not in another. Justifying anger is the same as protecting anger. You don't want to stuff it, you want to unleash it. Anger must have air to breathe. Punch holes in your tightly closed bubble of emotions and let the anger out.

GUIDELINE 1: If you feel it, say it. Sure, you may stumble over your words, choose the wrong words, or sound silly. But so what. Trust your words. Just let the words flow out of your mouth without censorship.

GUIDELINE 2: Speak your mind (using the DESC method) at the time you feel the anger. Don't wait until later. There's never a better moment than the present—even if you can come up with 100 reasons why *right now* is not appropriate. Forget it. Right now is just fine. It's *how you say it that makes your anger okay at any time.*

GUIDELINE 3: Treat anger like a new experience. If you've never let yourself feel sensations of anger, go for the challenge. But start slowly. Experience anger in different ways. For example:

    a. Start with your words: say critical, disagreeing or angry words.

    b. Change your voice inflection: go up, down, or escalate the tone in a slow stair-step fashion.

    c. Let your body get tense. A little tension is okay. Too much tension will make you want to yell.

    d. Look the person straight in the eye.

    e. Stay *in* the situation.

GUIDELINE 4: Once you express anger, let it be. Don't be anxious to recall your anger, hoping to made amends with the person before it's too late. It's a horrible feeling, there's no doubt about it. But let it happen. Just walk away after expressing anger. Wait 15 minutes or a half-hour. You may be surprised. The person you were angry at may come to you to make up.

Protecting Yourself from Depression

Do you hate people calling you "Susie Cream Cheese?" Are you always happy-go-lucky? Is there always a smile on your face? The world could be overthrown by gigantic lizards and you'd be smiling—you'd smile and keep an optimistic outlook. And why? Well, it isn't because you really think things are hunky dory. It isn't because you're oblivious to world problems, your own problems or major crises in life. No. You know perfectly well that these things are happening. You know all too well, unfortunately. That's why you smile. You smile to lift the morale of other people, and hope they will like you for it.

That smiling and "Hey, things won't be so bad" attitude does something else. It prevents you from being depressed. You can't get depressed. You won't let yourself be depressed. You can't emotionally afford it.

Why not? Letting yourself be sad or mildly depressed sidetracks you from your perceived mission: your goal in life is to make others happy and not let them down, no matter what. You'd go to any extreme to keep things light and happy; to raise doubtful spirits to hopeful ones; to pull others out of the dumps and see them back on their feet. That would feel right. But there's a problem with this mission: how can you always feel happy and energetic enough to carry it off?

You can't. There's no way. And if you think you've been doing it—you're wrong. You've been faking it; faking it for a long time. That smile on your face is forced. You don't always want to smile. You don't always want to make other people happy. But something compels you to do these things: you do them to avoid guilt. You'll blame yourself if you drop your charade and let an "I don't care" attitude spill out. Guilt will eat you alive.

The other reason guilt eats you up is that you think you can't be selfish. You think you don't deserve to feel bad, feel sad, feel slow or do anything that reduces your daily speed. Other people do, you don't. Your fears go something like this: If I let myself feel sad or slow down ...

- who will run the household?
- who will take care of my spouse?
- who will take care of my kids?
- who will help out at the church or synagogue?
- who will keep us on budget?
- who will make sure things in general get done?

Nobody will, of course. If you don't do it, you absolutely feel nobody else is capable or willing to step in for you and get the job done. Possibly this comes from experience getting sick or feeling in the dumps and being expected to keep up that "I can do everything" image. Possibly you stop people from helping you when you feel sad, bad or sick; you don't want them doing things they don't know how to do. They will only screw up, and that will make more work for you later. Whatever the reason, you just don't let yourself be depressed.

How not to protect it. You can't go your entire life pretending depression doesn't exist. We all get sad. And you're no exception. You may think you're a martyr—that you rise above sadness and despair and keep the energy going. But that's a lie. And it's time to tell the truth. So ...

GUIDELINE 1: If something makes you sad, say it at that moment. "It makes me sad that you ..." No sugar-coating the words. Just let it come out right from the heart.

GUIDELINE 2: Listen to your body. If your body wants to slow down because you're feeling tired, sad, or sick, go with the body. Tell others you're doing this. Then do it. It's one thing to say, "I'm going to lie down," and another thing to actually do it. Make good on all of your promises. Once you follow-through the first time, people will know you mean it.

GUIDELINE 3: Let other people (friends, family, spouses) help you when you feel down. It's not imposing on them. It's not shirking your responsibility. It's not going to destroy their approval of you. But it *will* teach people you deserve special treatment.

GUIDELINE 4: Let things that *should* get done not get done. It won't kill you. It won't create havoc for long. In families or relationships where there are no helpers and all the things you typically do go on hold, let those things stay on hold. Don't do them. Even resist doing them if the family and spouse get annoyed and start accusing you of being lazy or not living up to your duties. By "not living up to your duties," you will force them to go hungry, go without clothes, and live in chaos until they start pitching in. That's the fastest way to change people's behavior. Remember, you can only get people to do things differently if you inconvenience them first.

Sharing Control

You now get the gist of how to let go of control. You don't need it as much as you think you do. It was a crutch. And it didn't work anyway. Things always backfired. So, let's put control out to pasture. It's time to share control to make sure other people in your world are there for you when you need them. Put people in a spot where they can't possibly say, "Sorry, I don't want to help you," or "Hey, you've done it right for so long, why should I get involved now?" You show them how to get involved right from the beginning.

Force others to do for you

Deliberately ask family, friends, and spouses to do something for you. Your favors will vary, of course. Nothing too large, nothing too small. Don't ask them to do things they've never done or have no idea how to do. Don't figure, "Hey, if I can do it, so can they." Wrong. You do too many things they don't know how to do, don't want to do, or will think you'll be after them if they do wrong. Follow these guidelines, to start.

> **GUIDELINE 1:** Ask the person to do what he or she already knows something about or already does at a bare minimum. Stick with the person doing this minimal amount for a couple of days. Then, increase the amount.

> **GUIDELINE 2:** Ask the person to try doing some new things you normally do for them. Make it a show-and-tell. Don't expect them to pick up on it the first time—not even the second or third times. Keep your standards low. Keep your criticisms down. And keep your patience high.

> **GUIDELINE 3:** Follow a new rule when people do things for you: it's neither the quality nor the quantity, but the effort that counts. It may seem a cheap excuse for their blatant goof-ups and forgetfulness, but so what. There's a more important goal here. That goal is getting people who are not used to doing for you to start, so you can share control.

Let others do for you

You can ask family, friends, and spouse to do favors for you. That's the good news. You still feel in control because you initiated the request. But what if you don't initiate the request? What happens if these people surprise you? What if they take the initiative and do things for you without your reminding them?

"Then I'll feel like I'm a helpless nothing and they have to care for me!"

That's right. You'll feel that they're treating you like an invalid. You'll feel angry, resentful, and suspect foul-play; they must be up to something. You smell ulterior motives all over the place. "Nobody just does these things for me on their own. What's the catch?"

What if there isn't a catch? The danger is that you'll look for an ulterior motive until you find one. The problem is, the one you'll find may only exist in your mind. None of these people created it. None of these people acted on it. In fact, it was the farthest thing from their minds. So, if it's real, it's because you put it there. You've set them up to look bad. It's called *entrapment*. You've proved to yourself that they were dishonest, and confirmed in your mind that nobody really is willing to do things for you.

By canceling out other people's efforts, you're preventing the very thing you want the most. You can beat this self-fulfilling prophecy by following these guidelines.

GUIDELINE 1: Thank people for anything they do. Don't tell them why they didn't have to do it or even promise to do things for them when you feel better. Just leave it at "Thank you."

GUIDELINE 2: Accept the reasons people give for helping you.

GUIDELINE 3: Invite them to do more for you after they have done one or two things. Don't be shy; don't be modest. Be upfront with requests.

Limit your responsibility

How much you do for people is an index of who you are. Even though it shouldn't be. You do one favor, you're a great person. You do two favors, you're a greater person. You do three favors, and watch out—they won't know what to do with your greatness. You'll shine all over the place. At least in theory you will.

In truth it goes a little differently. Do one thing and you're appreciated. Do two things and you're taken for granted. Do three things and you're expected to do four things. Do many things all the time and you become a slave. Then you think of yourself, not as a hero, but as a prisoner. Who you are cannot be based on what you do or how much you do. That gauge simply doesn't work. It's biased. It breaks down. And you'll never really win by looking at it that way. The answer instead is to limit how much you do for people. Limit your responsibility to things you (1)want to do, (2) can share doing with others, or (3) must do for yourself.

That *must* may get you in trouble. It's easy to turn anything you don't really have to do into a "must do." You simply force yourself by guilt into doing it. But you don't have to do that. Stop short of being a full-time do-everything-for-others person.

GUIDELINE 1: Say *no* when asked to volunteer on additional projects.

GUIDELINE 2: Ask to step down from existing responsibilities. You won't lose face if you are diplomatic. Just explain that you're too busy or don't want to do it anymore. You are entitled to change your mind.

GUIDELINE 3: Delegate. Tell people in your family you want them to do routine things. Show them how. Walk them through it. But make sure they do it. Set up IFs and THENs to motivate them to do it. Positive IFs and THENs always work better than negative IFs and THENs. For example, "If you set the table, then I'll sit with you for a couple of minutes and watch TV." Naturally, be sure you follow-through on your promises so they take your IFs and THENs seriously.

Let others figure it out for themselves

Control also takes the form of rescuing. That's something you're not doing anymore. You already retired your lifeguard uniform and do not have to rush into the water to save every drowning victim. It's left up to another person. Either the victim himself or somebody else can play lifeguard. Put your desire to put a person at ease on hold. You can't do it. You won't do it. And you'll probably feel the outrageous effects of GWs for not doing it. GW—that's "Guilt Withdrawals." You'll feel every kind of guilt imaginable. You'll blame yourself; you'll blame other people; you'll make up excuses for why you should step in and put out the forest fire.

But hold on, Smoky, nobody asked you to do it. Let the person on fire find his own fire extinguisher.

GUIDELINE 1: When you hear a cry for help, don't be a superhero. Silently, count off 10 seconds, while you stay right where you are. Don't move. Don't volunteer to "be right there ..." Stay put. Wait for two things to happen.

1. Wait for the person's aggravation to escalate. It goes up and then it goes down. This happens quickly, and you mustn't mistake the person's rising frustration as anger at you. Nobody is angry at you. Don't assume this person is angry at anything you did or didn't do.

2. Let somebody else step in, or let the person figure it out himself.

GUIDELINE 2: When directly asked, "Can you help me?" don't jump to be a troubleshooter. Make the person work harder to solve her problem. There are several ways to do this.

- Prompt the person to ask questions about the problem.
- Prompt the person to figure out solutions.
- Praise the person for acting on that solution.

GUIDELINE 3: Let the person make mistakes along the way. You know how much you hate mistakes. And you probably think people hate mistakes as much as you do. Maybe they do. But you can't worry about it. Permit people to trip over their own feet by saying and doing things that don't add up. Let them make fools out of themselves if it's a learning process. They may hate it, but that's tough. They'll learn from the experience.

Be a talker

Part of controlling is saying nothing. You make people feel good by limiting your comments to "uh-huh," and "gee, that's awful." You nod your head, turn it sideways, and shrug your shoulders. But your ideas remain hidden. That's not good. Habit or not, it must change. You need to be a talker. You need to interrupt the speaker when she's midway through her words. Interrupt right when you've had a thought or want to express your opinion about something. Don't delay. Don't evaluate your words before saying them.

Part of sharing control is to participate in the conversation.

GUIDELINE 1: Listen to what is said. Choose a key point and give your opinion of it.

GUIDELINE 2: Make the person respond to your opinion by saying, "Well, what do you think about what I just said?"

GUIDELINE 3: Prevent yourself from listening too much. Say over and over again to yourself during the conversation, "Have I expressed my opinion?" A good rule to follow is this: one comment per minute of conversation. That comment should be original: fault-finding, disagreement, or clarification. No make-the-person-feel-good statements are allowed.

Be a listener

Okay, let's switch gears. Here's the opposite situation. Say you're always giving your opinion. Not only do you interrupt, but you tend to monopolize the conversation. It feels normal. You're not trying to be mean; in fact, if somebody tells you you're talking too much, it deeply offends you and you stop talking immediately. You're not deliberately overtalking. It just comes out that way.

So, imagine how tough it is to put a muzzle on your mouth. You know you should say less, but the compulsion to lead and direct people is overwhelming. It's like a craving for ice cream—you want it now! That's the hang-up. You're not used to delaying satisfaction. And no one else is used to seeing you wait, either.

You can't wait. You feel that if you don't give an opinion from the onset others will hate you, think you're incompetent, or completely reject you. You also fear others will say or do things that are wrong, and you can't bear to see them make mistakes or suffer grief afterwards.

Others can't wait. Suppose you try waiting. You deliberately hold off giving an opinion. That doesn't mean others will let you put the brakes on. Family, friends, and spouse accustomed to your initiative-taking efforts are not about to let you off the hook. They've come to expect you to lead them down the path toward enlightenment. Why should today be any different from yesterday? It won't be, unless you disappoint them.

GUIDELINE 1: When a person starts to tell you about a problem, just listen. Shake your head up and down when agreeing and side to side when disagreeing, but say nothing.

GUIDELINE 2: When instinct tells you to chime in, bite your lip. Hold your tongue an extra minute. Don't spoil the suspense. Don't let out the answer just yet—maybe not at all. Keep it inside.

GUIDELINE 3: When you're asked, "Well, what do you think?," just shrug your shoulders and say, "Gee, I don't know." Of course, you're pretty sure you do know the answer and you'd love to tell him, but pretend you don't.

Go ahead, say what you're thinking right now. You see a problem with this exercise, right? You think there's something contradictory going on here, don't you? One moment you're being told to speak at will and express your opinions. And two minutes later you're told you should hold back and say nothing. What's going on here?

Here's what's going on. The general rule is *go ahead and say what's on your mind when you want.* But if you're a person who always speaks up, always mixes in, and always solves other people's problems and feels this is your duty in life, take heed: your general rule is *hold your tongue when your impulse is to speak.* Let others do more of the talking.

Let somebody else take the lead

Are you notorious for chairing different volunteer groups? Knights of Columbus? Lioness Club? Rotary Club? Sunday school committees? PTA? You name it, and you're in charge of it, right? Of course, right. That's the only way you'd volunteer to do things. Letting somebody else be in charge feels funny. It is a risk. You're risking this person will have no idea what to do and the whole project will be a bust. And guess who'll look stupid because this group failed under bad leadership? You will, right? At least you think you will.

You insist on taking the helm to prevent mistakes and keep others from ruining your image. You can't bear mistakes and are afraid to trust anybody. So you don't trust. You simply volunteer to be the president, organizer, chair or leader. If others want the job, you find an unusual way to persuade them, trick them or turn events around so you can become the captain of the ship. It's sneaky and clever; and it always works.

For example, you may offer to be an assistant to the leader. But you do so much of the project that others in the group start listening to you, not the designated leader. Or, you might start bad-talking the leader behind the leader's back, either to others in the group or to higher-ups in the organization. If they believe you, you get the job because you're on top of things and the other person—so you say—is "not in touch."

But really, you're the person who's not in touch. You're trying to make up reasons to stay on top. That's exactly what you don't want to do when you shed control. Get rid of that need for power by learning a simple way to be a follower for a change.

GUIDELINE 1: Decline the offer to be in charge of a group. Just be another groupie.

GUIDELINE 2: When you see what needs to be done, hold in your opinions. Let the leader or other group members figure it out. They will figure it out soon enough, if you let them. You may dislike their solutions, but so what? Let their solutions stand, unless they require you to do something personally offensive. But that's not likely to be the case.

GUIDELINE 3: Do as little as possible to get by. You're used to killing yourself with effort and working late hours. But not anymore. Let other people do that. It will feel odd—and terribly selfish. You'll resist it initially, thinking that people perceive you as a hard worker and now you're shirking your duties. "My God, that will damage my reputation forever!"

Let your reputation be damaged. That's what you want anyway. You want people to begin viewing you as a team player, not a hero or heroine. You don't want to be commander-in-chief.

Don't be double and triple safe

Like the proverbial elephant, you never forget anything. You can't afford to forget. All it takes is one absent-minded error and everybody will know you goofed. And goofs make you look incompetent. But only when it happens to you. How well do you handle mistakes other people make? About the same as your own mistakes? Not very well?

Preventing your own errors is one thing. But making sure others don't make mistakes carries this too far. You may also feel worried: if that person makes a mistake, she might blame me for it. That's a double justification for giving your input. You don't want to be caught off guard with an "I told you so." And then there's a third reason: people in your past always made a certain mistake, so you're sure this person will make the same mistake. The result is excessive reminders.

Excessive reminders. You want to be double and triple certain that people dot their I's and cross their T's. They are to know ahead of time all obstacles to a goal and troubleshoot solutions to those obstacles. You expect people to be completely aware of every right way, wrong way, and in between way. No exceptions permitted. No gray areas tolerated. Flexibility doesn't exist. It can't exist. You didn't grow up with flexibility: things were rigid. Flexibility was for weaklings or people who couldn't get their act together and be organized. But not you; you say you're organized; you say you're a planner; and you'd swear if you took the lead, everything would go right.

That's why you remind people too much about things. You even remind them of things you really know they know. For example, for 10 years your husband has awakened earlier than you and made you coffee. It's Thursday night; you're feeling vulnerable. Out of your mouth comes the reminder, "Are you going to make me coffee tomorrow morning?" You have no faith that he'll do it. You feel you can't take the risk of trusting things will go as usual.

Here's another example. You're on a trip with your wife. She is driving. You let her map out your route, against your better judgment. She gets lost. You don't handle it well; in fact, you lose it. "What's the matter with you? Didn't you review the roads ahead of time so you'd know where you're going? If I had done it, we would't be in this mess!" The truth is, however, you hate doing it, because you're likely to make the same mistakes as your wife.

In a nutshell, here are the reasons you give people so many reminders:

- You're not used to things happening routinely. You've come to expect things randomly, or erratically, or when you'd least expect changes. This has caught you off guard in the past and caused great shame.

- You anticipate the person doing something stupid—making a mistake—and it will embarrass or shame you.

- You anticipate the person forgetting, and it will mean you'll have to do what he forgot to do.

- You can't stand seeing another person make a mistake. You hate it when you do it, and you hate it even more when it happens to somebody else. You may even blame yourself for their errors.

- You're used to being criticized and over-reminded by your parents, so you think it's the natural—even loving—thing to do in a relationship.

Is there any way to stop giving so many reminders? Can you learn to trust friends, family, and spouse? Yes, but it's not easy;

not because they don't deserve it, but because your deeply instilled habits compel you to correct, overcorrect, and agonize over the threat of mistakes. Still, here's what you can do when you feel you want to give a reminder.

> **GUIDELINE 1:** Ask yourself, "Does this person already know this? Have I seen this person say or do the thing I want to remind him about?" If so, don't say anything. That way, if he forgets or makes a mistake, he must deal with it himself.

> **GUIDELINE 2:** Ask yourself, "Has the person really committed a horrible crime for forgetting something or making a mistake?" Probably not. Let him make the correction on his own. Your rubbing his nose in it accomplishes nothing, except to make him angrier.

> **GUIDELINE 3:** Tell yourself, "Let it go." You can try trusting the person. You may feel something bad is about to happen. Or, inside you're feeling anxious just keeping your thoughts to yourself. There is no harm in expressing this frustration as a point of self-awareness. Say, for instance, " You know, I'm feeling really scared inside about what you're doing, but I'm going to let you do it anyway." The other person will receive it better. Hearing your feelings is a lot better than hearing criticism.

Find ways to do nothing. This is a tough one. You feel that by always doing something, you're in control. You can prevent bad things from happening if you're out and about and spinning your wheels in every direction. You'll clean the house. You'll do the chores. You'll still work your 8 hour job. And, you don't know how you do it, but you still find time to call all your friends at night. Hustle and bustle—that's your life story.

Yes, you're coming and going all the time. But why? Why are you always on your feet? Here's why: you don't want to sit down. You don't want to stop. That would mean you're lazy. That would mean you're helpless. That would mean you're a sitting duck for criticism from others who hate seeing you relax. So, you're not really in control by keeping busy; you're actually running scared. You're too afraid to watch TV, and too anxious to do only half of your daily projects. You can't imagine slowing down.

Break the cycle.

GUIDELINE 1: If you don't have a job, set aside 1 hour in the middle of the day to sit in front of the TV and just relax. Of course you'll feel guilty and absolutely wasteful. You're supposed to feel that way. If you're getting nervous just thinking about it and even more nervous when you try it, *then you're doing it right.* Let yourself go through natural guilt withdrawals. If you do have a job, be sure you take your morning break, lunch break, and afternoon break. You're entitled to them by law.

GUIDELINE 2: Try doing things in slower motion. Think of it like tip-toeing around a person while he's trying to sleep. Slow, softer movements replace harsh, rapid movements.

GUIDELINE 3: Every evening, set aside one hour for doing something that is personally relaxing. Read a book or watch TV. Be careful not to do "busy work" while relaxing. No knitting while watching TV; no talking to business partners on the telephone while snacking. Confine yourself to the one personal activity. No other distracters are allowed.

The need to control gradually lessens when you deliberately try to break its chains. But those chains have been on for a long time and sometimes feel like just another layer of skin. You don't even notice they're there. That's why you need to go against what feels normal. Put the guidelines in this chapter to work for you, and Step 8 will be a breeze.

STEP 9
No More Feeling Hurt for Other People

> *I cry so easily,*
> *And I don't know why.*
> *When his stomach aches,*
> *My body shakes,*
> *When he feels bad,*
> *I feel sad,*
> *And all I want to do is cry.*

Your greatest gift is your worst enemy: being so sensitive. You're sensitive to everything. It's like you have satellite antennas picking up on other people's feelings. You can feel them, experience them, and know exactly what a person must be going through. You *become* that person. All because you're a short-wave receiver for human feelings. Far reaching cries for help come in loud and clear. You'll tune them in, decipher their distress signals, and step into their miseries as if they were your own. You do it naturally, without much thought. That's what makes it a gift.

What makes it your enemy is that you tune in to people who abuse you. Persons on the receiving end of your short-wave radio love to have you decipher their messages. "Go ahead," they feel, "it's all yours." So, falling for the bait, you decode their messages one by one, examining them with a fine-tooth comb. So much effort goes into decoding the message that you feel like you know the messenger. You feel for him. You hurt for him. And you want to help him relieve his hurt—that way you can relieve yourself of your hurt. Except, it isn't hurt that you're feeling. What you feel is guilt. You feel guilty that somebody else is hurting and you're not helping them.

Step 9 can help you fight this unusual type of guilt. It's the need to feel sorry for other people out of your own sense of shame and guilt. It all begins with a simple problem: You can't stand to see somebody hurt. It bothers you to no end. You believe people are naturally good and that nobody deserves pain. Pain also reminds you of the terrible pain you experienced in childhood. And you don't want to repeat that pain under any circumstances.

So, how can you break this compulsion to take on other people's pain? Do you have to get rid of all your compassion? Isn't a little compassion a good thing? Of course it's good. The trick is balancing a healthy dose of compassion with compulsive compassion. That is what you'll learn to do in this chapter. So, let's get started.

Why Feeling Sorry Is Really the Result of Fear

You just heard news of a friend's aunt's death. Death of any sort bothers you. You don't like talking about death. The whole topic makes you nervous. And, because it was your friend's aunt, you feel worse. You send your friend a sympathy card. You call your friend offering to help the family. You even take precious time off from work to attend the funeral—and you didn't even know his aunt. But it didn't matter. You know your friend. And you don't like your friend feeling pain.

Why is this? Why can't somebody suffer pain or bad news without it affecting you? Are you a glutten for pain? Do you look for hurt in others and gravitate toward it like a magnet? No, of course not. That's because you get all choked up over good things as well. It doesn't matter whether you're seeing the birth of your niece or the death of an animal on *National Geographic,* tears roll from your eyes. So what's going on here? You're feeling good or bad because of *fear*. Not phobia-like fear. But a different kind of fear. Fear that makes you:

- *Remember bad things* that have happened to you—you hate to see other people or things experience sadness.
- *Feel helpless* against the cruelty of life. You perceive of yourself as a victim in much the same way as the person who's suffering.
- *Feel sadness* when something good happens. You feel it's only a matter of time before good things are replaced by disastrous or self-damaging things. You become pessimistic. For example, seeing the birth of a fawn upsets you because you fear that some hunter will shoot it before it matures to a full-grown deer.
- *Feel envious* because you never experienced such delight. For example, you envy children playing on a swing set nearby. Why? Because your parents never bought you a swing set. They never made your childhood so happy. Or, if they did, something always ruined the fun.

Other types of fear interfere with feeling sorry for people. Here's what they are and how to stop them.

Afraid of not being loved

You draw upon a person's emotions to get closer. Telling the person you can *feel* for them enlists their support and may make them want you more. They love you because you relieve some of their hurt.

How to say "It's okay." It's okay to risk not being loved by letting a friend agonize over troubles herself. Stay out of her emotions. You weren't invited into them. If you are, then show compassion for a brief time, cutting it off after 15 minutes. Beyond 15 minutes and you're already trying on their emotional clothing. Don't make the clothing fit. It doesn't fit you, and it won't fit you unless you work hours at it, tailoring it to your personality.

Afraid of being hurt again

You can't stand pain. Childhood memories of pain give you shivers up and down your spine. The yelling, screaming, spanking, conflict, and chaos all vividly return like a horrible nightmare. You don't want to think about these memories for long. It upsets you too much. That is why you can't stand seeing other people go through pain. It reminds you of your pain. Pain, grief, or dying. You hate these things with a passion. But you can't ignore them, so you fight these haunts with the only weapon you have: sensitivity. You figure that if you can step in and relieve another person of some of the pain, that's less pain you'll have to feel.

How to say "It's okay." What happens if you don't intervene? Can you suffer re-plays of fearful, painful memories without helping anyone. Yes, you can. You don't have to make that person your personal tranquilizer. It's okay to refrain from sharing your woes with him. It's okay to let him undergo pain and suffering by himself. When you do that, be sure to physically walk away, so you won't keep staring at him and wondering, "Would it make a difference if I said something?"

Afraid of hating yourself

Fear of shame is the ugliest one. You're afraid that if you don't show any concern, you will be rejected and you'll feel ashamed of not looking out for others. This type of guilt gets added support from many religions and cultures who push doing for others over doing for yourself. For example, Catholic-raised people learn very early in Sunday school that tooting your own horn and ignoring brotherhood is sinful, and Hispanic-raised females are expected to cook, clean, and care for their elders until they reach a marrying age. Personal ambitions go on hold out of respect for their parents.

How to say "It's okay." So, is it okay to violate your religious or cultural heritage to feel emotionally alive? Sure it is, because you're not really violating the religion or culture per se. You're just bucking one of its *implicit* practices—a practice not in writing but generally understood by all of the members. This doesn't mean you're sinful or disrespectful; it means that you're flowing with the times. Today many of these customs and practices do not fit life as we know it. We live in a selfish world, not a selfless world. Men and women equally are striving for careers and have high ambitions. You can still be loyal to a culture and a religion when you adapt their standards to the realities of modern living.

Absorbing Feelings

The bottom line, however, is this: "How can I stop compulsively absorbing other people's feelings?" Methods used to break this habit will seem the phoniest you've tried so far. You'll really say, "This does not feel natural." And that's okay. It won't feel natural because it's not natural. You've never blocked any of your feelings before, or only for a short time, because it triggered enormous guilt. Now is the time to learn how people who seem caring, but not overly compassionate, do it.

How to stop crying when others cry

STEP 1: When you feel initial sadness or happiness, step away from the person, place, or thing for 3 minutes. Regain your composure.

STEP 2: Detach yourself by saying, "It belongs to that person, place, or thing. It's not mine, nor does it have anything to do with me." Do upper body relaxation exercises for a minute or two.

STEP 3: Return only after feeling composed. Look at the person, place, or thing repeating STEP 2. If you lose it and start crying, repeat all three steps again.

STEP 4: Resist making the person who's crying feel good. Let him cry. Crying may be healthy for him. At a funeral, for instance, crying is normal. Let him cry as part of natural mourning.

How to stop crying when anything sad or happy happens

After you try the steps above, try these steps as well.

STEP 1: When you feel tears starting, stand back and say to yourself, "Those things happen in life. It's okay for good and bad things to occur. I'm not to blame. God's not to blame. Maybe nobody is to blame. It just happens."

STEP 2: Choose a behavior opposite to crying, for example, laughing. You can do it, but it's awfully hard to laugh and cry at the same time. Or another behavior— asking questions. You ask questions when your "thinking cap" is on. You're curious, inspecting, and problem-solving. Let's go back to the funeral example. Ask your friend's relatives, "How did his aunt die?" or "Was it a long illness?" Such questions are perfectly normal, perfectly healthy, and prevent you from absorbing the emotional temperature in the room.

STEP 3: Tell yourself you did a good job. It's critical to do this. Don't just brush it off by telling yourself "People are supposed to do this," or "It's about time I got my act together." Nonsense. You're handling your emotions *now*—that's what counts. Forget how it should have been. Live in what you're doing right now.

How to stop living through another person

You have a unique and separate body. You have your own heart, lungs and brain. You breathe and think like nobody else. You never were, and never can be a carbon-copy of anybody else. So you must stop living through other people. This is called *channeling*. It's like the spiritual form of channeling. In the movie *Ghost*, for example, Whoopi Goldberg played a psychic who communicated messages from a spirit ("Sam"). She was the only one who could hear the messages and relay them to the mortal world.

You act like a channeler by experiencing other people's emotions and relaying them to your own world. Unlike the Whoopi Goldberg character, you don't let go of your channeled emotions and return to your natural self. Instead, you replace what there is of you with these newly acquired emotions from another person, and they become your new emotional identity.

Well, maybe that's the way it was—but not anymore. Let's move on to ways of getting rid of that emotional identity. You want yourself back. You want to think and feel for yourself and by yourself. No intrusion of others' feelings is acceptable.

STEP 1: Say to yourself, "Those are their feelings, not mine."

STEP 2: Stay out of the situation that their emotions seem to draw you into. For example, seeing your girlfriend happy, you find yourself feeling happy and wanting to do something with her. STOP. Don't go with her anywhere.

If you do, you'll be riding on her emotional coat tails. Delay going with the person at least for 30 minutes. During that time ask yourself how you feel about what's going on. Talk to the person about your feelings. Once you announce how you feel, that instantly cuts the umbilical chord. If you decide your feelings are different, that's okay; go with your feelings. Don't do things with the happy person just because you think you're supposed to be happy.

STEP 3: Ask another person to feel what you feel. This sounds like reverse psychology, but it really isn't. You can break the leader-follower routine by reversing the roles. You become the leader and let the other person be the follower. Request that the new *follower* hurt as you hurt or feel happy when you feel happy.

"Wait a minute! This sounds like I'm creating a channeler out of this person. I don't want to do that, do I?"

No, you don't. And you won't. Other people who are naturally less emotional than you are can benefit from a surge of power once in a while. They need to build up their sensitivities to other people. No matter how much caring they show you in STEP 3, be prepared for it not to last long. Just as you work hard to stop being so sensitive, they have to work twice as hard to become more sensitive. It's ironic, but true.

As your behavior changes, your feelings of emotional self-worth will also change. Remember that who you are is not gauged by how much you feel for others. There are other indexes of personality more reliable than feelings. Liking yourself is one of them. You can celebrate reviving yourself from a long sleep—a sleep that has lasted many years. Now you're awake, refreshed, and independently feeling what belongs to only you. No more feeling for others. At least not without some strings attached. When they feel for you, by all means, return the favor.

STEP 10
No More Repeating
Bad Relationships

Nobody loves me,
everybody hates me,
guess I'll go eat worms ...
—Author unknown; circa 1890.

Don't I ever learn from my mistakes? How can I get it through my thick skull that this type of person is dead wrong for me? So you try again. You look for all the warning signs. You feel bad vibes and put your protective shield up. That's what you think. You think you have this relationship roller-coaster licked. But you don't. You get burned again. This time it hurts even worse.

You get burned in relationships a lot. Sometimes three times. Sometimes many times. But each time the same problem recurs. At the beginning things start off great. But that doesn't last. Soon familiar patterns creep back into the relationship, stinging you like a wasp. Even when you've been stung, you let things stay the same. You don't call it quits soon enough. You want to. But you just don't do it.

Why is this? Why do you repeat bad relationships? In Step 10 you'll come 180 degrees from feeling victimized and out of control. No more of that feeling. Now you're in control—healthy control. You've advanced tenfold. You can see clearly what people do to you, how you let them do it, and why you'll never let them do it again. Sunshine fills your life. You can see hope and promise. You move in directions that feel right and *are* right.

But can you do all this alone? Being alone is a tough nut to crack, and you've just about cracked it. Still, it's natural to want a companion. You deserve somebody to love you, and know you'll give a great deal of love in return. So, where do you start? In bars? In single groups? In church or synagogue activities? Or, do you put an ad in the newspaper for a companion? All these routes may produce some answers. Single people do exist. And they want the things you want: love, affection, and loyalty. The problem isn't always finding the right partner. The problem is knowing *when* you've found the right partner.

Many things you're about to read will sound familiar. Some parts of it more familiar than others. But one reaction you're bound to have is this: "You've got to be kidding!" You may not like knowing the person you're currently in a relationship with or would like a relationship with is really bad news for you. You may not like realizing that Mr. Right or Ms. Right always has been there in the wings—but you dismissed this person because of feelings that scared you. You now discover they were healthy feelings.

What you will like is the control you have from knowing how to spot good and bad relationships. No waiting three weeks, a month or a year for results from the lab. It's 24-hour turn-around time today. You'll know as fast as you can pinpoint certain characteristics. No digging or probing into past history is necessary. It's all laid out for you—neatly—on a platter. All you have to do is look at it and know what you're looking at.

Stop Sign on "Comfortable" Relationships

Suppose you meet somebody and instantly feel you've known him all your life, and you can't believe how comfortable you are around him. Just talking to him gives you goose bumps all over. It's like magic from the start—as if this relationship were made in heaven. "Amazing—he likes everything I like and we're so much alike, I can't believe it."

You're hooked. You've been drugged by the same aphrodisiac that did it to you before in another relationship. This time, though, you say it feels different. This time "She really is the right one for me." You know it; you feel it up and down your spine. Inside you're so self-assured that nobody is going to change your mind. It feels so definite. "Yea, I'm positive about this guy—he's on the up and up."

Are you sure about that? Are you 100% positive this person is completely different from all the other bad-news relationships you've escaped from in the past? Let's put your intuition through a test.

1. List the particular characteristics of this person that you like.

_____

_____

_____

_____

Now circle YES or NO to the following questions:

2. Do these characteristics make you feel at home?

　　　　　　　YES　　　　　　NO

3. Do these characteristics make you love him more?

　　　　　　　YES　　　　　　NO

4. Do these characteristics make you think about this person a great deal, maybe obsessively?

　　　　　　　YES　　　　　　NO

5. Do you feel this person needs you?

　　　　　　　YES　　　　　　NO

6. Do you admire how this person has advanced through rough times to semi-good or good times?

　　　　　　　YES　　　　　　NO

7. Does this person make you feel young and playful, or bring out your hidden strengths and talents?

　　　　　　　YES　　　　　　NO

8. Does this person let you talk most of the time?

　　　　　　　YES　　　　　　NO

9. Do you love listening to this person?

　　　　　　　YES　　　　　　NO

10. Do you look past any minor problems saying to yourself that it's nice to be loved again?

YES   NO

Okay, let's score the answers. If you circled 8 out of 10 *YES*, your relationship is headed for the same type of trouble you've had in the past. You're falling for the same lines and actions, and developing the same soft attitude of "Oh, it's okay, everybody has faults." You're letting this person build up a dependency on you, or you're depending too much on this person. Whichever way the pendulum is swinging, somebody is going to get cut—and soon.

So, stop the pendulum right now. Start by memorizing the *comfortable rule*.

COMFORTABLE RULE

If I feel perfectly comfortable around a new person— girlfriend or boyfriend—and start settling into a relationship, that means I'm doing things that are familiar to me. And if they're familiar, then I've done them before.

You've said or done these same things many times before in relationships that failed. You may not recognize these behaviors in current relationships, because you've conveniently forgotten all of the early courting days of each of the past bad relationships. All you remember are the rotten times. And that's what most people remember. But, *think* for a moment.

- Didn't my last partner say those things to me when we first dated?

- Didn't my last partner buy those things for me when we first dated?

- Didn't my last partner promise me those things when we first dated?

- How many other characteristics are similar to those of my other partners when I first dated them?

You are very comfortable with this new person, and much about him feels familiar, because you're saying and doing many of the same things you've done before. But remember, if you've done them before, you've done them in relationships that didn't work.

"No, wait a minute. That's not true. This guy is really different. He really loves me. He really cares for me!"

That's right. He really does. He really cares for you, loves you and will do things for you just like they all did in the past. It's just that, right now, you like feeling wanted. And you don't want to give it up so quickly. This all-absorbing love replaces your loneliness and puts blinders on you. That's what happens when you smile all the time because you think everything is going perfectly. Unfortunately, everything's not perfect; you're walking down the same dead-end path once again!

The Separation Trap

If you're in a not-so-good relationship and want out, is there a way out? Probably, but the options look dismal. First, you could lie your way out of it: "I think I need more space." That's sure a big lie. And lying makes you feel guilty about hurting the other person. So, lying is out. Second, how about dating another person while you're still in this relationship? That sounds reasonable, since you're at least not hurting your partner, right? Dead wrong. That's bound to fail as well. There really is no easy way to slide out of relationships other than doing the dirty work of facing the facts. You'll just have to tell the person exactly how you feel.

But we're getting ahead of ourselves. Let's go backwards for a moment. Consider why the other ways of ending a relationship backfire all the time.

Now that I've got you, I don't want you. Your relationship may lose speed and feel like it's going nowhere. The excitement of chasing this person with phone calls, surprise visits, impulsive gifts, and inching closer to that ultimate kiss is done. You've caught the sucker. You've won your prize. If getting her into bed for a romping night of sex was the goal, pat yourself on the back for a job well done. Captain, you've made it. Land-Ho!

Your conquest took days, months, possibly a solid year of hard, intensive labor coupled with certain strategies. The strategies paid off and your goal is behind you. But so is the excitement. All that adrenaline-rushing vitality building up the suspense has been lost. You don't view the person in the same light anymore. That sparkle fades to a blur. You lose your *lust* for the person. Interest disappears because you survive on making others feel good or helping others. When the job is done, so is your relationship. And you feel it's time to move on.

Here's what to do instead.

Ask yourself:

1. "Why does my relationship feel stale?"
2. "Why don't I have an interest in this person anymore?"

Some of the answers may surprise you:

1. She has her act together and doesn't need me anymore.
2. She's too independent.
3. He's too boring.
4. She's doesn't help me grow.

Essentially you're saying this person either is "fixed" and your nursing role is over, or the relationship is stagnant. You're tired of the "same-old-same-old." The problem is not that this person is boring, because you are attracted to boring people. They may be more of a challenge, or they may be less of a challenge. It's whichever is easier for you to conquer. You need to interrupt this cycle before you get involved with anyone new.

The grass is always greener on the other side. Okay, so that's not what you do. You don't look for a new tournament once your relationship begins. But you certainly fantasize about new relationships, don't you? Curiosity eats away at you. You wonder whether partners in other relationships are enjoying themselves more than you are. And there are lots of people who fit in this category. Therapists, siblings, parents-in-laws, brothers and sisters-in-law, cousins, and best friends. "Yeah, I'll bet they get along better than we do." You compare their relationships with your own, point by point.

- Let's see, he goes out with his wife twice a week, while we do it once a month.
- He buys his wife flowers on Valentine's Day, while my husband thinks Valentine's Day is stupid.
- Those guys make love every night. We're lucky if "we get it on" once in 2 weeks. And it's lousy at that.

The *comparison-game* gets obsessive. You're dying to know more about that person. You become a detective. You eavesdrop on his personal telephone calls. You pass by his desk and look at what's on top of it. You buddy-buddy up to him and let him disclose personal stories to you. Every day the information gets juicier. Data builds up. You log it in your memory banks, believing every bit of what he says he does and how he does it.

And then the real contest begins. If your world doesn't match up to his, you've failed. And you won't fail, because you hate failure. So you start shaping and reshaping your relationship until you do things like this other person does. If your partner resists, you get angry at him or her. If your partner consents, all the better. You're not in love, you're in competition. *You want to win this battle.* And why? Because being as good as the other person means you're not missing out on anything. You don't have to be jealous of the grass on his lawn because you've put the same grass on your lawn.

You can't stand feeling you're losing out on something. You want the best house, the best car, the best deal, and nobody will do it better. Because if someone does, you'll feel cheated. And that's exactly the horrible feeling you had during childhood; the feeling you swore you'd never experience again.

There's nothing wrong with a competitive edge. It's great for racquetball or tennis. But not in relationships. Relationships are not a one-upmanship sport. You don't improve your relationship by outdoing another relationship. Like gambling, you have to know when competition has to stop.

Here's what to do instead.

- Turn to your partner and ask what he or she likes about you and the relationship. Use internal guides to determine what the relationship needs instead of seeking guides from other relationships.

- When competitive thinking gets obsessive, turn it off by doing exactly the opposite of what you feel compelled to do. For example, you want to have sex five times a week like Susan and Tom. You already do it twice a week. Okay, shift gears. Now you'll prompt sex once a week. Deliberately defy your desires.

- Stop cozying up to him for more information about his life. Put your curiosity to rest. When temptation rises, walk away from it. You don't need it, and you don't want it. It only feeds your obsessions.

Mistaking independence for abandonment. You're loyal to the relationship, and you're pretty sure your partner is. But something keeps bugging you. Something has changed. Your partner doesn't call you as much. Your partner doesn't spend as much time with you. Or, you're living in one part of town and your partner lives in another part of town—or out of town. Physical distance between the two of you is growing. You can't rush over there for a quick visit. The drive is too far. The long-distance calls get too expensive. Your partner gets farther and farther away from you—and you feel abandoned.

For example, Ruth and David dated for 3 years during college. They saw each other almost every day and spent many nights together. In her senior year, Ruth transferred to another college on the other side of the state. They kept the relationship going by telephone and visited each other every weekend. Both knew this separation was a healthy, mature step, and believed the relationship would get stronger because of it. But things broke down. David panicked. After 2 months he started thinking Ruth really didn't want him, that he was losing her love. Ruth thought he was crazy, but David disagreed. He felt awful about himself; he had no one to care for him, to build him up when he felt gloomy, and to make him feel masculine.

So David looked around for another partner. He secretly dated a couple of girls, getting that burst of "God, I'm great" feeling so he could get through the week. Then it hit him. After every date he became more depressed hating himself for cheating on his girlfriend. He would call her up accusing her of having affairs and not loving him enough. Again, Ruth didn't know what planet he was on. Twice he broke the relationship off with Ruth and twice he patched it up.

David's dilemma isn't just a "guy" thing. Distance between two people, for whatever reason—work, relocation, or just daily schedules—makes both people more independent. They don't need each other as much. They don't want each other as much. They begin to enjoy their independence. You may agree in theory: "Sure, independence is where it's at." But in practice, you think it stinks. That's because you're not viewing it as independence. You're viewing it as abandonment.

Pulling your love cord out of the socket makes you lose your electric charge. You feel empty, depressed, and ashamed. Shame can be reversed in several ways. But not by forcing your partner to reaffirm her love. That only reaffirms your fear that nobody, especially this partner, really loves you. Instead, try these steps.

Here's what to do instead.

- Increase the distance even more. Call less frequently. Write less frequently. Visit every other week, or every third week. If it's the time schedule at fault, designate at least one time slot per week to be together. That's all you need. Your goal is to encourage independence, not to stifle it.

- Resist all impulsive quick-fixes. They only make you feel good for the moment. Your booster shot of affection or flattery only lasts for a day. Then it turns ugly—heavy guilt. You'll feel ashamed of your disloyalty, ashamed of your vulnerability, and ashamed of causing this person to abandon you.

Afraid to let go of Number 2. Suppose you can't do it. You can't break off that secret relationship, because it just feels "too good." But you don't want to hurt your primary partner. Night after night you wrack your brain for ways to make both relationships work. You love your partner; you'd do anything for him. But you also love this new person. He excites you in ways never experienced before. Maybe it's the way you have sex with him. Maybe it's how he talks to you. And he gives you just what you've been looking for. "How can I give it up?"

You can't. At least not with a snap of your fingers. It's tougher than that. You're afraid to let go of partner Number 2. Partner Number 2 holds love magic over you, and you can't bear to see it go down the tube. Letting the relationship slip through your fingers may mean the worst of all possible worlds; the paralyzing fear that: "Something this great may never happen to me again." It will be gone forever; just be a distant memory. You'll never reclaim it.

Holding on to Partner Number 2 relieves this fear. You're afraid of losing the prize. But really, you never had it to lose. All you had was a booster shot of something that felt nice because you weren't dealing with your troubled partner directly. You were trying to repair the troubled relationship without touching it.

No relationship can survive when you are two-timing. It just won't work. Loyalty is a two-way street without any detours. Another person diverts you from this course. You feel aloof. Detachment gets worse. You feel apart from your partner, and begin feeling pity for him. Now you see him as a pitiful creature. "Oh, how sad for him." You're up on a high pedestal looking down on this person you once loved. You cannot repair your primary relationship by holding on to both partners.

Here's what to do instead.
   1. Begin by telling Number 2 it's time to stop having sex. Stop touching, kissing, hugging and everything else that goes with affection. Lay off the physical candy. Go without it like you're on a starvation diet. No cheating. You can't afford to cheat. One slip and you've returned to that fake feeling of security.

2. Partner Number 2 may send you on a guilt trip. "You mean after everything I've done for you, sacrificed for you, you're now telling me it's over?" Resist the punch line, "If you really loved me, you'd tell your partner to hit the road." Let these roadblocks pass. You don't need them, and you're not going to fall for these old lines.

3. Take another inventory of your primary partner. That doesn't mean jumping feet first back into a bad relationship. Just reconsider whether you're making the right decision in ending it. Ask your partner how he feels about the relationship, and whether there are things both of you can do to improve it.

4. "Okay, fine. Maybe it's salvageable," you say, "but should I tell him I cheated on him? This one is up to you. Some experts say it's okay to be honest. Some say that things in your affair may actually help the relationship between you and your partner. But there's a down-side to letting the cat out of the bag. It's called *disaster*. By revealing your secret, you may kill the relationship forever. If that's what you want to do, okay, go ahead and spill the beans. But if you're trying to make things work, think again. You can explain that you've felt disloyal lately and have wanted the relationship over, but in fairness need to get your partner's views first.

You'll get more than his views. You'll probably get an outpouring of honest and insightful thoughts about the relationship and where it's headed. And that's good. You couldn't have asked for anything more.

Make a clean break of it. Can you just say *good-bye*? See you in another life? It sounds easy, doesn't it? Mouthing the words in front of the mirror even looks easy. You're just telling it the way it is: No bones about it. You're being upfront, direct, and honest. At least that's what you have in mind. You're tired of jumping through hoops. You're tired of making up excuses why the relationship should continue. You know it's finished, and all that's left is to announce your decision.

So what's stopping you? Fear. Fear that he will hate you. Fear that he will be upset. Fear that he will hate himself. Fear that instantly sends you into shame-land. Overwhelmed by guilt, you stutter, look fidgety, and bail out at the last moment. Hated is one thing, but knowing you're about to cause grief in a person or make him feel abandoned is unthinkable. You'd hate it if somebody did that to you, so why inflict this torture on somebody else? Why? Because part of building healthy relationships is learning to say good-bye. Ending a relationship builds independence. You realize that the person is no longer around for support. You can't run back to him at a moment's notice. It's over. Finished! You're on your own.

So, make a clean break. You don't have to spend hours rehearsing your lines, but you may want to structure your farewell speech in five steps.

Here's how to do it.

> **STEP 1:** Tell him you want to talk person-to-person with him, not on the phone or through a letter.

> **STEP 2:** Once there, sit down next to your partner, facing him. Enumerate everything you like about him. Don't make them up. Be truthful. Remember, there were qualities you found attractive about him initially.

> **STEP 3:** Now shift the conversation to the subject on your mind. Identify each of your problems, without going too deeply into them. Just name them. Skip the analysis. You're not his mother. You're not his therapist. And no matter how concerned you really are about him, just keep the focus on specifics. Just tell him the facts.

> **STEP 4:** Point out how difficult it is to deal with these problems. Explain that:

> > • "I don't really want to deal with these things."

> > • "I don't really know how to deal with these things."

> > • "I feel these problems interfere with my growth and career."

> > • "I feel we're moving in different directions."

- "I feel uncomfortable staying together for the sake of having a companion."

STEP 5: You've said your piece. Now go home. There is no reason to make this last *date* a romantic one. No last flings. Preserve your dignity by kindly excusing yourself from the situation and leaving. You'll be much happier if you don't fall for internal shame-messages telling you to buffer his hurt feelings. It's okay to let him hurt. Hurt is part of change.

Nobody loves me,
everybody hates me,
guess I'll go eat worms,
big ones, juicy ones,
even itsy bitsy ones ...

The Rebound Trap

Guilt is horrible to experience alone. You've just broken up with a person after many months, many years, or worse—after investing a major chunk of your life in a relationship. And for what? What did it give you? Grief? Heart-ache? Did it teach you never to trust a partner again? At first, sure, that's what you feel. You hate the opposite sex. It burned you. And you never want another experience to make you feel so low, so inferior again. Never again.

Distrust is like a cold. It's awful while it controls your body. You can't think straight. You can't walk straight. And all you want to do is hide. Hide from who'll remind you that you have a cold. But like a cold, distrust finally goes away. Either it disappears before you make the actual split with your partner or it happens about 1 to 2 months after the split. Distrust turns to curiosity as loneliness creeps back into your life. Loneliness makes you feel scared, deprived, and empty. You suddenly panic.

You wonder, will anyone:
- ever find me attractive again?

- ever want to marry me again?
- ever want to deal with my habits again?

A surge of nostalgia hits you between the eyes. "Maybe I was too hasty to break up with this partner—perhaps we should mend the fences." So you ponder getting back together. You might even call once or twice, testing the waters to see how he'll react. You're building up false hope, not for reconciliation, but to relieve your empty feeling.

And then it bombs. He has no interest in repairing the relationship. You feel devastated and have to return to the chalkboard. This time you don't have a clue as to how to begin again. Until, a new person enters your life.

If this New Person is somebody you dated during your marriage or relationship, the person is still there but takes on a new role. But if this New Person is really a *new* person, life just entered the Twilight Zone. You're headed down *rebound lane.* "Rebound" gets its name from many games, like basketball or pinball, where a ball bounces off stationary objects and into other objects. It doesn't stay in one place. It's in constant motion. You might be like that ball. You had one relationship and now you're bouncing to another relationship, not because you really love this New Person, but because this New Person is a rebound from the old person.

Rebound relationships start for the many reasons discussed above. They stay together because of shame and its accompanying guilt. Guilt is a great adhesive. Hardware stores should carry it. Guilt solidifies the relationship even when you have serious doubts about it. But before you know it, it's too late. You feel stuck—royally—without a dime to call home. You can get so deeply entwined in rebound relationships that you can't get out no matter how hard you try. Trying gets you nowhere. Why is this?

The reason is that you stay in the rebound relationship for the wrong reasons. You stay in them for affection, for guilt, to protect the other person, and for secrecy.

For affection. Rebound relationships with the New Person endure because you're "eating something" that's been out of your diet for years. It's called *affection.* It tastes good. It feels good. And you want more of it. You get a lot of attention. The New Person listens you to you when you need him. The New Person consoles you and is your advisor. But that's only one side of the coin. The other side feels better. It's the intimacy you really like. Passionate love-making puts your mind at ease. It rebuilds your confidence. It relieves your loneliness. You're now receiving the attention you've missed, both physically and emotionally.

And it is addicting. Daily doses of hugs, kisses, and sex can feel so good that you don't want to let go. Telling yourself, "I really love this person," can be deluding. You're rapidly falling in love with what this New Person does for you. You're reacting to supply and demand. You demand a high dose of physical love, and this New Person is right there supplying it for you. It's a perfect arrangement.

Or so it seems. But, perfect relationships never occur. This is no exception. Physical affection misleads you into thinking the relationship possesses a certain magic never felt before. You've come under the spell of affection. It relieves you of shame, of thinking of past bad times, and affection helps you overcome fears of starting over again.

Here's what to do instead.

Keep on the look-out for these warning signs:
- Always making love whenever you see this person
- Activities that revolve around or ultimately lead to making love
- Obsessively thinking about making love with the New Person

Interrupt these unhealthy behavior patterns by following these guidelines.

FIRST: Stop making love so much. It sounds funny, but take this advice literally. For this relationship to have a fighting chance, you must diversify activities with this person immediately. Do other things. Talk about other things. Let several days pass without making love with this New Person. Learn to enjoy this person's company without relying on physical comfort.

SECOND: Delay calling or sending gifts to your New Person whenever the thought pops into your head. Intuitively it feels like a sweet gesture; something you'd love somebody to do for you. But it will backfire, and you probably followed those same instincts with your previous relationships that didn't work out. So, instead, wait until you see her before expressing your feelings.

THIRD: Ask yourself, "Why do I need affection from this New Person?" Track down the stresses in your life that cause this need. Are they at work? Are they from not resolving another relationship? Are they physical problems? Pinpoint what you think they are and then talk to the New Person about them. Let your New Person be your sounding board. Ask for his or her opinions, rather than medicating the problems with affection.

To avoid shame and protect the other person. There's another reason you stay in new relationships: You feel sorry for the other person and are afraid to hurt her feelings. Avoiding shame, you'll do anything to blunt the impact of her getting burned. Suppose, for example, that you really want out of the rebound relationship, but sense the split will distress your lover. You'll chicken out—Not because you don't believe in what you're doing, but because you're afraid to let another person feel grief on your account. To spare her grief, you come up with irrational reasons for continuing the relationship.

- "Well, I really don't know this person well, yet. I should give it time."
- "This person has been through a lot. I don't want to cause more grief."
- "There really is a good side to this person. I just have to be more patient."
- "My standards too high. This person is probably fine."

Such reasons create the illusion that *you're at fault for the way things are going.* Blame shifts to you to relieve the other person of blame and to protect the other person from feeling sad. Protecting the New Person gets more complex as the relationship develops. At first it was "I didn't want to end the relationship." Now it's "I really need to show I care about this person." Shame, in other words, mobilizes you to patch things up for even *thinking* you caused this person grief. Any small thing the New Person wants is your command. Inconveniences they cause in your schedule get more frequent. One day your beeper goes off with his phone number on it. You call him in a hurry, thinking it's an emergency. But no, he just wanted to say *hello*. The next time it's more than a hello. Now he wants you to come over for dinner. But you already had plans for dinner; well, at least you did have plans. You change your dinner plans to accommodate him.

Interruptions in your life increase to satisfy the every whim of this New Person. You're even worrying about when he'll call you next. Sometimes you deliberately take your beeper off and leave it off. Other times you don't return the calls. However, small delaying tactics get you nowhere. The moment that telephone or person-to-person contact resumes, you're there, rushing around to please the New Person.

You wanted a new relationship, not a repeat of the old relationship. You don't want to always be saying *yes* and constantly seeking approval.

Here's what to do instead.

First, ask your New Person to put out his own fires. You're not the local fireman. Your job in life is to watch out for yourself, first. And if there is time leftover, maybe you'll help out your New Person. This will make you sound selfish, but it's no more selfish than your New Person is being. Balance that selfishness and control. Let your needs take priority by refusing to be mobilized by his anxieties.

Next, make a point of disappointing and disagreeing with your New Person. Prepare for conflict. Have *words* with him. Arguments on a small scale break the ice quickly. You'll also see how effectively both of you can handle arguments. If you and your New Person panic, consider the relationship finished. If both of you sail through it after being direct and honest, you just bought another month of the relationship. There's still more evaluating to do.

For secrecy. The biggest problem with a rebound relationship is knowing when to make it public. Relationships that develop during a marriage are naturally kept secret, but so are relationships that develop during separation or right after a divorce settlement. That boundary of space and time, around which emotions are bouncing and you're either a basket case or looking for comfort, is called the *vulnerable zone.* In the vulnerable zone you don't know if you're coming or going— you're terribly confused and you don't like yourself very much. So the last thing you're going to do is announce to the world that there's another person in your life. It would cause more questions, more problems, and more grief.

Secrecy keeps a relationship going. You hide behind the wall of silence while another you—the happy you—is out there partying. You can't tell people about this New Person because of fear. You're afraid that people will ...

- think that this is the reason you're ending your marriage or relationship. Never mind that your partner verbally or physically abused you or that you tolerated his indiscretions for 20 years. "All people will see is my infidelity and think that's why we broke up."
- think that "I'm the bad person and my partner is the good person." You can't stand the idea that he'll be liberated in people's eyes. You'll be viewed as the black sheep, the devil stirring up trouble while your partner will enjoy the publicity as a victim.
- harass me and this New Person. They'll chase us down, and indirectly mark me with the Scarlet Letter. I'll be marked for life as a home wrecker.

Fearing these events, you keep a low profile when you date the New Person. You do things only at his house. No going out on the town. If you do, it's a town far away from your town. Even then, even if far away from the crowd, you're still looking over your shoulder wondering who's looking at you, who's going to catch you and report it to the rest of the world. Lurking in your mind is the thought that it's only a matter of time before the word will get out. And when it does, then what?

Does the relationship suddenly end? Does it all blow up in your face? No, just the opposite. You get more sneaky. You get more afraid. And the higher the risk of exposure, the less chance the relationship will go public. You grow so accustomed to this *private life* that it's hard to change it. Even after you divorce your partner, you still can't bring yourself to go public with your New Person. You feel it's too dangerous. The same fears still haunt you, and won't ever go away.

Secrecy is dangerous because you're avoiding things. You don't want people knowing what you're doing or why you're doing it, so you're avoiding people. Gossip about your relationship may start and travel through the community. But gossip isn't harmful unless you feel ashamed about it. And you'll feel guilty whether people are talking publicly about you or doing it secretly. You'll feel guilty just thinking people might do this if they find out. So, one way or another, you'll be feeling guilty. That's why it pays to come out of hiding if the relationship is a serious one.

Here's what to do instead.

- First, end the relationship you're cheating on. If it's already ended, wait 1 month before announcing your new relationship. That will give you time to determine whether the new relationship feels like a rebound.

- Introduce your New Person to good friends and your children—if you have any. Indicate to your ex-spouse in conversation that you're dating somebody new. Do the same if it's an ex-girlfriend or ex-boyfriend. Wait until you feel there is a solid adjustment to these people. Wait about 1 month. During this time go out publicly with this person.

- Introduce your New Person to your parents.

- Draw this New Person into your business or work life by attending holiday parties together or vacationing together at conferences.

- Have a prepared reply to rumors you confront or people directly asking you "Is he why you broke up with your husband?" You say: "That's really not important. I'm sorry you think it is. I'll be happy to talk to you about something else." Use the DESC to resist falling for their word-traps and shame-games. People are good at that. Watch out for slippery curves such as: "Don't you feel bad that you did this behind your ex's back?" Of course you don't feel great about it, but it's no one else's business. You don't owe other people an explanation. Let it go.

Separation and Divorce

Relationships go bankrupt for many reasons. But breaking up is tough. You don't toss in the towel and actually resign yourself to ending a relationship unless you really can't make things work. You'll know when this happens by two warning signs. First, trying only causes more trouble. And second, one day is good and the next day is bad; there's no consistency. You think you're making headway—one day things look wonderful. The next day you think you're on a roll—and then things fall apart and you're back to stage one. You're ready to give up again. You're thinking separation or divorce. Your friends encourage it. Your parents even offer to pay the attorney fees. But you can't go through with it. You just can't act on it. Not yet.

There's something holding you back from separation and divorce. Things in the relationship or in yourself worry you. You obsess over them. You tremble at the thought of seeing an attorney. Fear intervenes. You can't even consider life without this partner. You won't have it. And why? Consider these reasons you may have told yourself. For each one, consider ways to overcome the fear.

"I can't for the sake of the kids." You refuse to leave the relationship for fear of dismantling the Norman Rockwell

fantasy of a *family*. You want a *happy family*. Breaking it up, you fear, will cause irreparable psychological harm to your children and make them lose touch with family values. They won't know what a daddy is. They won't know what a mommy is. Friends who have mommies and daddies will seem strange to them. They won't be able to cope. And it will all be your fault.

There's another way to look at this situation. You're not breaking up the family. You're saving the family. Suffering through another 20 years of verbal and physical abuse, of alcoholism or severe anger, of infidelity, late-nighters, and your spouse not coming home—all of these problems can cause far more psychological damage in both the long- and short-run than a divorce. The divorce actually relieves your children from the stressful surroundings. They don't have to avoid and escape difficult situations anymore. They don't have to feel humiliated, embarrassed, or afraid any longer. They don't have to think they're the causes of your problems.

"I can't because of my parents." You may hold onto a relationship because your parents and everybody in your family likes your spouse. They think he's wonderful. Your parents say she's "The best thing that's ever happened to you." They won't let you forget it, either. Your folks stuff this idea down your throat whenever they get the chance. That spouse is "God" in their eyes. How can you defy God?

You really feel torn when there's another person. Now the guilt you feel is twice as bad. Here you want to share your personal dilemma with your parents, telling them your marriage is rocky, and all you hear day in and day out from them is, "You know, I think your wife is great." Well, so much for hoping your folks will understand. They won't. And you feel thoroughly stuck.

You can end a relationship with a person your parents and family love if you ...

- Tell your parents what you're doing and that you expect not to get their support. Don't look for it. Don't be disappointed when it doesn't come.

- Act on your decision. Waffling back and forth with your emotions sets you up as a target for your parents' criticism. You don't need their criticism and can avoid it by planning your strategy ahead of time and executing it efficiently.

Remember that one main reason that your parents and family adore your spouse is because she says or does things they like. That doesn't mean these things are necessarily good or healthy. It just means your parents find them likable. Think about it. Your spouse may drink and play cards with your mom. She may love going to the bars with your family. But you're sober. And that kind of fun doesn't feel right. It used to, but not anymore. But your folks still party like this. Just because your folks do it doesn't make it right. And it doesn't validate your spouse's behavior either.

"Three strikes and I'm out." You want out but there's a twist to the decision. It would be divorce Number 2. Or, maybe it's divorce Number 3. "Not again!" "How could I? What's wrong with me that I can't stay married?" Self-probing questions rip a deep hole into your psyche. Into those holes comes a flood of shame. You feel awful. "Who would want a person divorced three times?" You're afraid of instant rejection in the singles market: "Three strikes and I'm out!" So, you decide to stick it out to avoid the humiliation of another failure.

You must accept that the number of marriages or relationships you have is not a gauge of your self-esteem. Realizing that you're repeating bad relationships is insight that doesn't come quickly. It's not learned over night. Little by little, through trial and error, discovery takes place. You discover mistakes you made along the way; choices turned sour due to unfulfilled promises and becoming codependent. By the second or third marriage, however, the light comes on. You finally gain a better grasp of what not to do and are ready to begin again, doing the right thing. Never feel ashamed for taking the time to learn new things that can make your life feel better.

"I don't want to start over." There is life after divorce, but not if you don't want to start over. Couples who have been married, dated, or lived together since high school may not have the foggiest idea how to live without a partner. You never learned the basics of dating. You never survived on your own. You went from mom and dad's house to your spouse. Nothing in between. Socializing was limited. You did nearly everything together. Romantic glue held you two together. You were inseparable. Sexually you started very early with your spouse, and you wanted that relationship to be the only one you ever had. From here to eternity with one person. That's how you thought of it then.

But that thinking doesn't fit in your life now. You don't want to stay with this person forever. Not anymore. Except what's the alternative? Can you go to work? No. Can you change your job? No. Can you meet new people? Hardly. So, what do you do? "I have no idea, and it's too scary to even try. So, I guess I'm stuck." And that's where you leave it.

But, in reality, you're never stuck, you're just temporarily inconvenienced. All people suffer the I-don't-know-what-to-do syndrome. It's part of normal growth. Feeling ignorant about such easy things as striking up a conversation or going grocery shopping for yourself happens when you feel something is forever. But now it's not. Begin by taking inventory of what you can and cannot do.

STEP 1: Figure out your strengths and your weaknesses.
I can do these things perfectly well:

1. _____
2. _____
3. _____
4. _____

These things I'm not sure about, or don't know how to do.

1. _____
2. _____
3. _____
4. _____

Do you have more items in the second inventory? Sure you do. There's a lot more we don't know than what we do know. Don't get frustrated.

STEP 2: Who do I know that can help me do the things I don't know how to do?

Name	*How they can help me out*
1. _____	_____
2. _____	_____
3. _____	_____
4. _____	_____

STEP 3: Talk to these people in person. Ask them specific questions about an area you're weak in. Don't feel bashful. Don't feel ashamed. Take advantage of their knowledge. It's nice to gain insight, for a change, without hurting at the same time.

Nobody loves me,
everybody hates me,
guess I'll go eat worms,
big ones, juicy ones,
even itsy bitsy ones,
down goes the first one,
down goes the second one,
oh how they wiggle and squirm.

Criteria for Selecting New Relationships

Test your powers of insight. You've been stuck in a rut for too long, finding the same types of people and going nowhere with each one. It's a merry-go-round full of predictable ups and downs, with too many downs. You can't seem to stop the cycle, although emotionally you know you're headed for another crisis if you don't act soon. One more bad relationship really will put you down in the dumps. And you don't need that right now.

So, you lay back and just wait for the right person to come along on their own. "I'll know when the right person comes along—believe me, I'll know." You really think you'll know.

You'd swear on the Bible that you can pick out the perfect person, if you get the right opportunity. One opportunity—that's all you want. Fine, but you've had one opportunity. Your Ms. Right has passed through your life many times, and you never knew it. She was right there, and you overlooked her.

"No, it couldn't be. How is that possible? Wouldn't I know the difference?" No, you wouldn't. You'd look right through her, as if she was transparent. You automatically dismissed these people. They didn't have a ghost of a chance with you, because you felt uncomfortable with them and figured they were bad news.

UNCOMFORTABLE RULE

The first rule of changing your criteria is this: *It's okay to feel uncomfortable.* If you feel nervous, intimidated, or even inferior around somebody, thinking he or she is so much better than you, then you're probably onto a good relationship. He or she is not any better than you are, but his or her actions are making you learn new things you need to learn for a healthy relationship.

Things I do not know. "Talking to this new person gives me the creeps." Why is this? Does he drink too much? "No." Does he call you bad names? "No." Is he rude to you? "Absolutely not." Then what? "He does weird things like talk about theater and politics. He also wants to take me to a lecture on campus. How stupid. I don't like that stuff."

Wrong. It's not that you don't like that stuff. You don't know how to do that stuff. Activities he talks about seem boring because you've never done them before. You feel pretty stupid. And you hate feeling stupid. For instance, take his conversation skills. You're not used to talking at length about things. Most guys you've dated speak in monosyllables ("Yep," "Nope," and "Maybe"). Or, the guys talk all the time—about themselves. But not him. He wants you to talk *with him.* He's sharing the floor with you. Your views are of interest to him And that scares you, because you suddenly feel ignorant. "He knows much more than I do, and I'll bet he'll think I'm a dunce."

You're not a dunce, you're just afraid. You're terrified because you can't respond to him comfortably, like you have with other guys. So, rather than focus on your own faults, you take the easy way out. You disqualify this person for being too smart, too talkative, and too odd for you.

And are you ready for the irony? Just yesterday you insisted to your best friend that the next guy you go out with will be intelligent, a gentleman, and have his act together. "I'm not settling for any more Mr. Macho Macks. He's got to have brains or forget it." You swore that to be true. And you've just eaten your words. That guy you hastily dismissed for being weird precisely fit the bill. Your words of promise fell by the wayside because, although you can describe this person, seeing him in the flesh prompts old habits to surface. The way you talk, walk, laugh, and handle interactions all come from a string of relationships that went bad. You know they went bad, but that's not enough. Just because you know they went bad doesn't mean you've changed how you act in relationships. You're still acting the same way.

Your words, your body language, and you're overall behavior send a powerful message to "stay away" to the healthy person. You're accidentally pushing away the healthy person and drawing the unhealthy people like flies to honey.

Things I don't know how to handle. One reason for reacting the wrong way is because you don't know how to handle the behavior of a healthy person. What do you do with it? It feels strange. You've never had to deal with it before. You've never seen it before. You've only read about it. And now here it is. You don't want to blow it, but you feel completely paralyzed and ashamed.

Using the skills you're learning in this book will do more than eliminate guilt. They will prepare you for relationships with healthy people. Asserting yourself, drawing attention to yourself, being selfish—all of these actions are normal for healthy people. It only stands to reason that healthy people of the opposite sex will now be attracted to you. Your behaviors now match their behaviors. Similar people attract each other. Forget the old adage "opposites attract," that's nonsense. You're far from being opposite to new people who want to know you. Alike in many ways, you're bound to encounter more diverse and interesting types of people you never thought might take you seriously.

That's when you must really pick and choose accurately. You may have licked the *uncomfortable rule* and can deal with things you don't know or don't know how to handle. That was the hard part. Now comes the easy part. This is where you learn to determine within seconds whether a person is appropriate or inappropriate. Is this person a high risk or a low risk? You'll know the answer immediately.

A, B, C, and then some. Choosing a relationship is like buying a car. It's a selective process. You go through natural steps before making a decision. First you read about the cars ahead of time. Second, you watch them advertised on TV, or just notice them on the road. You don't just impulsively pick one that feels good. Third, you figure out your expenses. Fourth, you take the car for a test drive, and then you mull it over a day or two. Finally, you decide whether the car is affordable. If it is, you'll buy it.

That's the way relationships should be. *Are they affordable?* Do they get you the emotional mileage you want at the price you're willing to pay? A higher emotional price tag on a relationship may not provide you with the fulfillment that a lower emotional price tag can offer. It's all a matter of risk. With cars, reference guides are used to help determine the risk. The *Bluebook* and dealership trade-in guides point to car values. But is there such a thing as a *psychological bluebook*. Does it do the same thing? Does it rate the worthiness and risk of relationships before you enter them?

Yes, there is. A psychological bluebook can pinpoint particular high risk and low risk behaviors of your partner, predicting how healthy the relationship will be. High risk behaviors warn of unhealthy relationships. You can expect the same old problems surfacing in a matter of time. Low risk behaviors predict the opposite: healthy interactions. Talking, sharing, and caring all become easier. You're less likely to step back into a caretaking role, a codependent role, or wind up feeling victimized. This time, nobody gets hurt.

High risk and low risk behaviors appear in the chart below. Look at this chart for a moment. It's an unusual psychological bluebook.

Criteria for Healthy Relationships

IF YOU FEEL UNCOMFORTABLE ... THAT'S GOOD ... STICK WITH PERSON A

Person A	Person B	Person C
ASSERTIVE	**AGGRESSIVE**	**PASSIVE**
Expresses opinions	Criticizes only you	Appears a "good listener"
Criticizes self and you	Boasts	Likes everything you do
Can be vulnerable	Not a listener	Discloses nothing personal
Admits mistakes	Makes demands	Edits remarks/apologies
Compliments self and you		Afraid to talk openly
Listens and talks		
FLEXIBLE	**RIGID**	**OVERFLEXIBLE**
Easy going	Can't break schedules	Gives in to pressure
Handles all people welll	Perfectionistic	Always agress
Good with all ages	Compulsive	Afraid of rejection
Offers to compromise	"My way or the highway"	
Looks for reciprocity	Blames you	
Adjusts to new situations	Never admits faults	
Asks for your help		
CONSISTENT	**IMPULSIVE**	**INCONSISTENT**
Say-Do (self-others)	Energy, but unpredictable	Afraid to do anything
Follows through	Prone to substance abuse	Appears lazy

Now, let's see how the table works. Most of your previous relationships were probably with Person B or Person C.

Person B. Person B tends to be *Aggressive*. That means he blames you for his mistakes, instead of blaming himself. He cannot listen well, and is always giving orders. Personally sharing his weakness is a *no-no*. He dares not expose his faults for fear of looking stupid or your knowing too much about him. He is also *Rigid*. Rigid people can't break their tightly structured schedules. Organization goes batty. Things must follow a specific order or it's *your* fault. There is nothing in moderation. Either it's black or white. There is no in between. "My way or the highway." This thinking is perfectionistic; mistakes are intolerable, and so are other people upsetting the order of his life.

He is also *Impulsive*. This can mean many things to many people. And unfortunately impulsive people can be misleading. Suppose, for example, you meet a person who is overflowing with energy. He walks and talks very fast. He's energetic, optimistic, always trying new things, a risk-taker. Things he does blow your mind. And his behavior is catching. You wouldn't usually order a pizza at 2:00 a.m. But when he's there, you do. When he's there, anything goes. You don't know what will happen from one day to the next. He's a three-ring circus filled with lots of surprises, and you're just sitting in the bleachers eating your popcorn and enjoying the show.

You're addicted to his excitement, because it comes at a time when life is boring. You want out; you want fantasy; you want to feel free. So, along comes Prince Charming with a bag full of tricks, diverting you from your boring life, and you're hooked. It feels good. It feels right. And you rapidly sink deeper and deeper under his control. When you're nostril-deep in quick-sand, you realize something is wrong. At first his surprises were fun. Now they're a pain in the neck. You don't know what he's going to do next. Everything is unpredictable. He says one things and does another. You can't plan ahead and you can't plan your life around him. That's when the "Oh-no, not again," feeling returns. You've been suckered into another relationship failure.

Person C. Okay, you've learned your lesson. No more impulsive "sweep me off my feet" relationships. You want somebody who has both feet on the ground. Along comes Person C. Faithfully, Person C smiles when you smile. She instantly conveys her feelings. You know she really cares about you; she listens to you and offers to help you with problems, without any strings attached. You don't have to do anything for her in return for her help. It feels wonderful. It's amazing. You're on top of the world. "Finally, somebody really admires me for who I am, without my bending over backwards for that person." At first you're in shock. "I can't believe this person likes me this much—there must be some mistake."

But there is no mistake. Cupid shot his arrow right through the two of you. Person C is gentle, compassionate, and easy going. You call the shots. Initially you regard her flexibility as a welcome relief from the rigid perfectionism of other people you've dated. "How nice not to be fighting all the time." Dating appears to go smoothly. You choose the theater, the restaurants, and even the afterglow. Your date is perfectly happy with any of your plans.

For 2 to 3 months the relationship flows smoothly. Then it hits you: "Gee, I don't really know what this person thinks—she always agrees with me or does what I want." Feeling selfish, you politely ask for her opinion and are told that "anything you do is really great." She flatters you endlessly, saying "I really have no complaints about anything you do." And you fall for it.

Two months later you notice a weird thing happening. Attempts to argue with her fall on deaf ears. She walks away or tries to patch things up. You get angrier and angrier, even shouting at her to "Open up and tell me what you think." But it doesn't work. Loudly, you insist that she stand up for her own opinions—and again the same result: silence. She says nothing and does nothing. You even start to notice that she doesn't follow through on many promises she makes to you. The reason she doesn't argue *(passive),* does whatever you want *(overflexible),* and doesn't follow through *(inconsistent)* is because she is afraid of conflict, criticism, and rejection.

Her fear of rejection resembles your old fear of rejection, but you didn't notice it at first. Now you do, and your next plan of attack is to end the relationship.

Person A. So, who is left? Person A. Is Person A the consolation prize? Do only relationship-losers settle for this award? Or, is it the other way around? Should Person A be the first type of a relationship looked for? Yes, that's the way it should be. Person A is your first choice for several reasons. This person forces you to accept new behaviors that are healthy and different from the Person B and C types. Person A literally prevents you from being the old you. You cannot possibly exhibit guilt-like behavior and continue dating Person A. He will spot it instantly and tell you about it, or end the relationship himself—you won't have to do it for him.

Person A is assertive.
- He says what's on his mind.
- He admits mistakes, and may also point out mistakes in you.
- He talks about himself and may sound selfish or arrogant, but he always compliments you as well.
- He listens to what you say, and may agree or disagree with it. His criticisms of you may sound cruel, but they're just honest opinions.
- He reciprocates. He'll do for you if you do for him. There's no one-way street here. He seeks a balanced relationship.

Person A is flexible.
- She can function in any situation and with most types of people.
- She takes minor risks and is not ashamed to admit failure.
- Nothing is set in stone. Disappointments are no big deal. She adjusts to life as it is. She can modify plans, adapt to new ideas, or accept alternatives. But she's no pushover, either. Part of compromise is telling you what she wants to do as much as listening to what you want to do.

- She asks for your ideas or advice. She regards you as a friend first, and an intimate second. This may feel strange, because if she doesn't want to jump in the sack with you right away or focus on your looks, you might think she's strange or not interested in you.

Person A is consistent.
- He does what he says he'll do about 90% of the time.
- He is loyal, but not to absurd levels. He'll keep a promise, but he'll break a promise, too. And you'll know it ahead of time. He doesn't leave things until the last minute. He's not into everyday surprises. That's why you find him boring. Lack of excitement may turn your stomach. It's not that he is unexciting, but rather that he is more predictable than Person B.

"Fine, so where am I going to find this Person A?"

This is the million dollar question. Criteria for a healthy relationship mean nothing unless Mr. and Ms. Superperson really exist out there. And you kind of doubt they do. You can't believe you've overlooked them. You've been up and down the dating boulevard for years and haven't spotted anything like Person A, right?

Wrong. You've seen Person A. You've talked to Person A. And you did the unbelievable: You rapidly dismissed Person A with a wave of your hand. He or she felt so wrong, so odd to be around, that you automatically lost interest. Person A didn't have a fighting chance. There was no way this person would enter your love-interest program.

That was then. Today is different. You are different. And you're ready for Person A to enter your life. You've stopped the guilt-routines. You've run through all ten steps of *No More Guilt* and can proudly look in a mirror and say, "Hey, I've licked the enemy." You've conquered haunts from the past even when you thought it was impossible. But nothing is impossible. People change all the time. And you just proved it. You proved that fighting the enemy within you can turn back the clock and recapture fun times, no matter how old you are. You feel alive, rejuvenated, and eager to get on with your life.

You're in control now. Your destiny is what you make of it. Ahead of you are easier days, no matter what problems you encounter. No matter what you do or who you do it with, shame won't bother you. It can't. Shame is fear. When you're afraid of things, afraid of people, and afraid of trying, then you'll feel shame. But that's not you anymore. You're better than fear. You've plugged away at these ten steps until they're second nature. Skills you now have prevent fear and prevent shame. There's no going backwards. There's no way you can be who you used to be. It's like riding a bicycle. Once you learn how to do it, it stays with you forever. From now on, be proud of the new you. Show yourself off. Announce your arrival to the world. And why not? You deserve the attention. And you deserve high praise for beating the guilt inside you.

Recommended Reading

Alberti, R.E. & Emmons, M.L. (1970). *Your Perfect Right*. San Luis Obispo, CA: Impact.

Ammer, C. (1982). *Getting help: A Consumer's Guide to Therapy*. NY: Paragon House.

Bradshaw, J. (1988). *Healing the Shame that Binds You*. FL: Heath Communications.

Breton, S. (1986). *Don't Panic: A Guide to Overcoming Panic Attacks*. NY: Facts on File.

Ellis, A. (1989). *Why Some Therapies Don't Work*. Buffalo, NY: Prometheus Books.

Ellis, A. & Harper, R.A. (1974). *A Guide to Rational Living*. North Hollywood, CA: Wilshire Book Company.

Friel, J. & Friel, L. (1988). *Adult Children: Secrets of Dysfunctional Families*. FL: Heath Communications.

Goldstein, A. & Stainback, B. (1987). *Overcoming Agoraphobia: Conquering Fear of the Outside World*. NY: Penguin Books.

Ruben, D.H. (1991). *Bratbusters: Say Goodbye to Tantrums and Disobedience*. El Paso, TX: Skidmore Roth.

Ruben, D.H. (1993). *Avoidance Syndrome: Doing Things Out of Fear*. St Louis, MO: Warren Green.

Ruben, D.H. (1993). *Family Addiction: An Analytical Guide*. NY: Garland Press.

Index

Abandonment, fear of, 11, 74-75

Advice, taking, 71

Aggression, 6, 36-37, 43

Anger, 13-15, 17, 43, 99
 guidelines for expressing, 128-129
 protecting yourself from, 126-128

Anxiety, 3, 15, 16, 79
 relief, resisting, 32-33

Apologizing, 1, 12, 17, 33, 50-51

Approval, 92-93, 109

Ashamed, 9, 10 *(see also Shame)*

Assertiveness, 60-65

Assumptions: about others, 29-30
 preventing, 30-33,34

Avoidance, 3,6, 9,16, 39, 43, 65
 definition of, 40-42
 solving, 48-55, 99
 types of, 42-48

Bad, guidelines for being, 108-109

Behavior, offensive, 61-64

Behavior profile chart, 24-25

Body: awareness, 96-98
 language, 99
 space, 53

Caretaking, 12, 177

Codependence, 114, 177

Comfort zone, 91-92, 113
 leaving the, 92

Compliments, accepting & soliciting,
 93-96, 98

Conflict, 15, 42
 negative, 55-60
 positive, 49-54

Control, 21, 92, 117-119, 135, 142
 sharing, 131-132, 136
 shedding, 138-139

Counseling, 93

Creativity, 112-113, 114

Criticism, embracing, 50, 121-122

Defensiveness, 9, 33, 37, 50

Defiance, 51-52, 110-111

Depression, 6, 19, 129-130
 guidelines for admitting, 131

DESC(*Describe, Express, Specify,
 Consequences*), assertiveness 60-65

Detachment, 69, 73

Disapproval, risking, 71-72

Distrust, 9, 44, 138

Divorce: family and, 170-172
 starting over after, 173-174

Doing nothing, guidelines for, 141-142

Emotional paralysis, 16

Escape, 6, 16 *(see also Avoidance)*

Extramarital affair, 58-59

F&F(Facts & Faults), 31-32, 37

Failure, fear of, 81-82

Favors: asking, 132-133
 limiting, 133-134

Fear, 6, 22, 69, 102-103
 and empathy, 144-145
 of hurt, 145-146
 of not being loved, 145

Feel-good tactics, 120

Feelings: absorbing other's, 15, 147-
 149

Flexibility, 13, 115, 139

Goals, inventory of, 111-112

Guilt: defined,1-3
 habits, 6-7, 9
 physical symptoms of, 2, 16, 76-79
 profile, 15-19
 chart, 24
 test, 19-23
 reversal of, 37-38
 roots of, 12-14

rules for fighting habits of, 4-7
situations, 4
six reactions of, 2-4
withdrawals(GW's), 134-135
   (see also Shame)

Help, asking for, 132-133, 174
Humility, 95
Hurt, facing need for, 68-71

Ignorance, pleading, 18
Imposter syndrome, 18, 81-84, 97
   reversing the, 99-100
In-laws, 104
Independence: vs. abandonment, 158-
   159
   developing, 113-115

Listening, guidelines for, 136-137

Marriage, 103-105, 110-111
Mistakes, 15, 115
   allowing other's, 88-89, 138-139
   owning your, 86-87, 102
   pride in making, 89

Okay Zone, 25
Others: absorbing pain of, 18, 143-145
   absorbing thoughts of, 27, 46-47
   analyzing, 28
   copying, 115
   criticizing, 50

Parents, 12-13, 22-23
   facing, 106-108, 171-172
Passiveness, 17
People pleasing, 2, 15, 20
Perfectionism, 84-86
Personalities: aggressive, 178-179
   assertive, 178, 181-182
   passive, 178, 180
Power *(see Control)*

Praise, accepting, 93, 95, 97
Procrastination, 45
Protecting others, 166-167
Put-downs, of self, 90

Questions, direct, 32, 34-38

Reading into others, 29-30 *(see also*
   Others)
Rebounds *(see Relationships)*
Reciprocity, 54
Rejection, 67-68
   vs. abandonment, 74-76
   defined, 124-125
   vs. disappointment, 122-123
   guidelines for embracing, 125
   stress from, 76
Relationships: bad, 151
   comfortable, 152-155
   comparing, 156-157
   ending, 155, 160-163
   healthy, 176-177, 181-182
   rebound, 163-170
   secret, 159-160, 168-169
   testing, 167-168
Relationships, new: criteria for
   choosing, 174-175, 177-178, 181-
   182
   feeling uncomfortable in, 175-177
Relaxation techniques, 76-79
   chart, 78
Reminders, excess, 139-140
   avoiding, 141
Rescuing others, 47, 134
   guidelines to avoid, 135
Revenge, 17
Risks, taking, 90-93,177,
Roadblocks, 34-37, 64, 69

Saying no, 51-52
Scapegoats, 11-12, 88
Self-criticism, 14, 27, 48, 75
Self-hate, 123, 127, 146
Self-love, 70-71

Self-protection, 119-120
Self-reliance, 113-114
Selfishness, healthy, 176
Sensitivity 143-145
    hyper, 46,
Sex: as medication, 17, 63, 165
    refusing, 103
Shame, 33, 38
    characteristics of, 9-11
    and families, 11-12, 103-107
    and friendships, 102
    and intimate relationships, 102-103
    (*see also Guilt*)
Shoulds, 3, 30
Siblings, 105-106, 127

Sorry, don't say your, 33, 50
Spouses, 104- 105,
Standards, lowering , 87-88
Starting over: after divorce, 173-174
Substance abuse, 16, 22, 58, 120

Taboos, 51, 101, 115
Talkers, 135-136, 137

Uncomfortable rule, 175-177

Visual imagery, 77, 110-111
Vulnerability, 6, 90-93, 168

Other Family Problem-Solving Books
... From Mills & Sanderson, Publishers

Nursing Home or Board & Care: Making the Right Choice, by Dorothy Kirk Ridge. Former state inspector of long-term care facilities guides readers in their efforts to find the best facility for their loved ones. Routed in the author's inspection experience, the book sets down in easy-to-follow terms a basis for determining a desirable facility from an undesirable one—always reminding the reader that it is the needs and desires of the loved one that really counts! $9.95

No More Guilt: Emotional Healing through Source Completion Therapy, by Robert T. Bleck, Ph.D. A Three-phase approach to putting past hurts to rest. Based on the notion that we must all (first) become fully aware of the true origins of our pain, (next) re-experience the original trauma, and (finally) complete the healing process by confronting the source/cause of our pain. $9.95

Recovering from Sexual Abuse and Incest: A Twelve-Step Guide, by Jean Gust and Patricia D. Sweeting. Two survivors collaborated to create this first-of- its-kind adaptation of the twelve steps of Alcoholics Anonymous to the unique needs of recovering victims of sexual abuse and incest. $9.95

Pulling Together: Crisis Prevention for Teens and Their Parents, by Dr. Harold D. Jester, with a foreword by Jacob Roseman, M.D. A veteran family counselor offers easy-to-follow advice to help teens and their parents learn to get along together and appreciate each other's good points. $9.95

The Big Squeeze: Balancing the Needs of Aging Parents, Dependent Children, and YOU, by Barbara A. Shapiro, Ph.D., with Vicki Konover and Ann Shapiro. An 8-step survival plan for dealing with the simultaneous needs of the three generations. $12.95

The Suddenly Single Mother's Survival Guide, by L. Patricia Kite. A modern-day guide to life after hubby, this delightful book is book informative and honest, offering advice on all that ails the single-again mother. $9.95

Childbirth Choices in Mother's Words, by Kim Selbert, M.F.C.C., with a foreword by noted childbirth author Carl Jones. These personal stories offer expectant parents a look at the various birthing options currently available in the United States. $9.95

Bedtime Teaching Tales for Kids: A Parent's Storybook, by Gary Ludvigson, Ph.D. You'll find no gentler way of helping young children (5-11) come to grips with serious problems than these 18 engrossing narratives intended to be read to the child at bedtime. $9.95

Winning Tactics for Women Over Forty: How to Take Charge of Your Life and Have Fun Doing It, by Anne DeSola Cardoza and Mavis B. Sutton. Written especially for those women jolted from the traditional marry-early, stay-at-home lifestyle by the women's movement, this book offers explicit advice on health, personal growth, financial planning, housing options, and more. $9.95

Place your order by telephone by calling 800-441-6224. We will gladly charge your purchase to your MasterCard or Visa. OR ... send a note telling us which book(s) you would like; enclose full payment for the book(s), plus $1.50 per copy for shipping/handling. **Mail your order to:**
*Mills & Sanderson * 41 North Road, Suite 201*
Bedford, MA 01730-1021